TRUTH MADE SIMPLE

AUTHOR'S NOTE

The Author had prepared four other Lectures, embracing the justice, the patience, the unchangeableness, and the incomprehensibility of God; but the size of the volume precludes their insertion. He mentions this, to show that he is fully aware that the Lectures here given do not embrace all that would be desirable.

TRUTH MADE SIMPLE

BEING A

SYSTEM OF THEOLOGY

FOR CHILDREN

ON THE

ATTRIBUTES OF GOD

JOHN TODD

SOLID GROUND CHRISTIAN BOOKS
BIRMINGHAM, ALABAMA USA

Encyclopedia Puritannica   http://www.puritannica.com
Project

Reformation Imaging Group   http://www.reformationimaging.com

Published by

SOLID GROUND CHRISTIAN BOOKS
PO Box 660132
Vestavia Hills, AL 35266
205-443-0311
solid-ground-books@juno.com
http://www.solid-ground-books.com

Truth Made Simple
The Attributes of God for Children

John Todd (1800-1873)

Cover work by Borgo Design. They can be contacted at
nelbrown@comcast.net

ISBN: 1-59925-077-2

TRUTH MADE SIMPLE

To *Master John Edwards Todd*:—

My dear Boy,

Most of this little book has been written and laid up in my drawer for a long time, because I was afraid to have it printed, lest it should not be good, and do good. Many a weary hour, long after you and most other people have been asleep, have I been working over these pages. Even now, I have many fears lest it will not be found to be all that I could wish.

If my plan may be carried out, I wish to make this series of volumes, (the last I ever expect to write for children,) a complete *System of Theology*, so plain, that children *can* understand it, so pretty, that they *will* read it, and so *good*, that it will make them good. The next volume will be on "the *Bible*," and *that*, I am sure, will be interesting—much more so than this can be.

You are now five years old, my boy; and should God spare your life five years more, I shall hope that there is not a word in this book which you, and all others of the dear children who read it, cannot easily understand. For children of your age, and upwards, I have written it.

You know how busy I am, and how seldom I have even half an hour to be with my children, because my duties are so many and so pressing. Should you live to grow up to be a man, and live—as I hope you will—to do good long after my head rests in the grave, you will wonder why your father, with all his professional duties, should ever write books. Let me tell you. Far away from our house, lives an aged widow. She has no children near her. She has no home. She has no money. She has been deprived of reason ever since I can remember. She does not even know her own children. That aged woman is your father's mother! For the last twelve years, I have had the honour to provide for this afflicted woman, and to do it, I have been obliged to use my pen. For this, I have written books, and every cent of the proceeds have thus been devoted. Nothing else would ever have made me an author,—nothing else would ever keep me one. Have I not done right? I charge you, then, my dear child, and I charge every child who reads this book, that if you live, and as long as you live, never fail to be kind, affectionate, and grateful to your mother. And if in her age she needs your aid, give it to her, though you work in a brickyard, or in a coalmine, to earn the money. Never let a sorrow dwell in her heart which you can remove, nor a grief which you can soften. Next to your God, let your mother have your love.

May that great Being whose character I have tried to describe here, ever bless you and every child who shall open this volume, making you wise, and holy, and happy. Then will the prayers of your father and their friend be answered, and then will he have a rich reward—the only one he can possibly have in this life.

Your affectionate Papa

CONTENTS

Can a child reason? Bolted door. New book. The text. Family visit. Dead brother. How to know about him. Pond. Bridge. Mill. Boat. Yard. Garden. Room. Sisters' treasures. Father's care. Application of the story. How we know about God. Two hard words used. Explained. Boy's hammer. Girl's doll. Greenlander reasoning. His kayak. The shipwreck. Marks on the sand. Reasoning. Barn on fire. The universe. What is chance? Its folly described. Story of man cast away. His island. Sees something. Description of it. Reasoning about it. A dialogue about it. Conclusion of the story. Beautiful house. Steps. Windows. Walls. Paintings. Not done by chance. Homer. His poems. Arabs' stories. City in the desert. Curious story of Columbus. Heap of watches. Heathen can know about God. Four remarks. First remark. Second remark. Third remark. Last remark. *The sequel.* Letter to Mr. Todd. The answer. The curious dream. Hafed. His beautiful house. His family. White peacock. Death of his wife. Death of his children. His wicked wish. His garden. A new world. Inhabitant. Dialogue. Description of the chance world. A chance man. His eyes. A chance sister. A young lady. Her features. A chance duel. A chance wound. Chance cattle. A chance herd. The happy owner. A chance sun. Measuring time. A misfortune. A house in the chance world. A chance feast. Effects of heat. Hafed's reflections. Hafed awakes. His views altered. Conclusion. *Spectamur agendo.* Lines on hearing this lecture.

Hiero. The heathen philosopher. His answer. God a rock. Why? God a tower. Hebrews want a word. *First reason why God called a spirit.* What cannot be seen. Angel visits. God a spirit. *The second reason.* The little dead boy. His death. God not heard. *Third reason.* The lightning. Holy Daniel. China. The absent brother. *Fourth reason.* Sodom's burning. The angel in Egypt. Angel in Palestine. Awful power. God's power. *Fifth reason.* What must die. What cannot die. *Sixth reason.* Angel students. Ignorance of a child. What angels do. What God knows. *Why God is unlike a spirit. First reason.* God had no beginning. *Second reason.* Angels have changed. A spirit learns new things. God does not. *Third reason.* A spirit limited. A spirit not in two places. Not so with God. *Fourth reason.* Spirits are servants. God not controlled. *Four things to be remembered. The first.* Pictures supposed. Why we make pictures. No picture like God. *Second thing to be remembered.* A good man's comfort. *Third thing to be remembered.* How God sees us. The dirty dress. *Fourth thing to be remembered.* The noblest thing. No picture of Christ. How Christ seen.

LECTURE 3.—GOD ETERNAL 61

The little boy and the pond. The broken arm. Sleepless night. A long year. The old man. Going backward. What eternity is—and God. How we measure eternity. How old is God. When eternity began? Mysteries. What we see begin. Will God stop living? The aged visitor. Rock in the ocean. What we learn. *The first thing.* What wicked men say. Solomon's brazen sea. Day of judgment. What is before us. *The second thing learned.* Great work. What it is. *The third thing learned.* The painted boards. Furniture. Houses. Great things. World to be destroyed. Golden knife. Why the world destroyed. *The fourth thing learned.* What we need not fear. Who will remain? *The fifth thing learned.* Why God is to be feared. His anger. Beautiful prayer.

LECTURE 4.—GOD IS EVERYWHERE 69

A question. How know we are here. How *men* see things. How *God* sees things. *First proof*—that God is every where. Abraham. Joseph. David. Jonah. Daniel. The furnace. African desert. Sailor boy. The poor soldier. Thomas Paine. The mountaintop. *Second proof*—that God is every where. Bible proof. Clouds. Storms. Mind. Sinning heart. Young raven's cry. God in heaven. God on earth. In all parts. *Special presence.* First example. Second example. Third example. The wind, the fire, and the earthquake. Fourth example. Awful murder. Mr. White. Beautiful description of it. The chamber. The blow. The deed done. *The secret.* Secret not safe. The anguish of spirit. *Conscience.* God in the conscience. *First thing taught by this lecture.* The eye that sleeps not. Story of Lafayette. The *eye.* Second thing taught. How God sees everywhere. The little cabinet. *The last thing taught.* The little seed. God present in troubles. God with the poor. The orphan child. Conclusion.

LECTURE 5.—GOD WISE 79

David. The soul wants a house. The soul's servants. The telescope. The eye more curious. How the eye keeps clean and safe. The frame of the house. The man of steel. The curious chain. The pump. Little channels. The house repaired. Witnesses against poison. The blood. The daily physician. Why we are born without dress. The elephant's head. The oyster. The muscle. The little bird. Birds wear spectacles. Little mill. Elephant's trunk. The reindeer. The whale's great coat. The clamp fish. Food prepared every where. The ship of the desert. The soft, spongy foot. The little songster. The shark. The pilot friend. Very small watch. The insect. The strawberry pot. Instinct. The young hen and the hawk. The beaver. How to build a dam. The bee. Infancy. Mother's love. The great basin. How rain made. The ocean a great blessing. Faces not alike. Men cannot write alike. The tongue and the ear. Day and night. The Bible. How proved from God. Jesus Christ. The wisdom of God seen. Who sees it. The world to be destroyed. New heavens hereafter. The little top. What God will do hereafter.

ADDRESS TO MOTHERS

NOW THERE STOOD BY THE CROSS OF JESUS
—HIS MOTHER.—John 19:25

Humboldt, in his celebrated travels, tells us, that after he had left the abodes of civilization far behind, in the wilds of South America, he found, near the confluence of the Atabapo and the Rio Terni rivers, a high rock—called the *"Mother's Rock."*

The circumstances which gave this remarkable name to the rock were these. In AD 1799, a Roman Catholic missionary led his half-civilized Indians out on one of those hostile excursions, which they often made, to kidnap slaves for the Christians. They found a Guahiba woman in a solitary hut, with three children—two of whom were infants. The father, with the older children, had gone out to fish, and the mother in vain tried to fly with her babes. She was seized by these man-hunters, hurried into a boat, and carried away to a missionary station at San Fernando.

She was now far from her home; but she had left children there, who had gone with their father. She repeatedly took her three babes and tried to escape, but was as often seized, brought back, and most unmercifully beaten with whips.

At length the missionary determined to separate this mother from her three children; and for this purpose, sent her in a boat up the Atabapo river, to the missions of the Rio Negro, at a station called *Javita.*

Seated in the bow of the boat, the mother knew not where she was going, or what fate awaited her. She was bound, solitary and alone, in the bow of the longboat; but she judged from the direction of the sun, that she was going away from her children. By a sudden effort, she broke her bonds, plunged into the river, swam to the left bank of the Atabapo, and landed upon a *rock*. She was pursued, and at evening retaken, and brought back to the rock, where she was scourged till her blood reddened the rock,—calling for her children! and the rock has ever since been called *"The Mother's Rock."* Her hands were then tied upon her back, still bleeding from the lashes of the manatee thongs of leather. She was then dragged to the mission at Javita, and thrown into a kind of stable. The night was profoundly dark, and it was in the midst of the rainy season. She was now full seventy-five miles from her three children, in a straight line. Between her and her children, lay forests never penetrated by human footsteps; swamps, and morasses, and rivers, never crossed by man. But her children are at San Fernando;—and what can quench a mother's love! Though her arms were wounded, she succeeded in biting her bonds with her teeth, and in the morning she was not to be found! At the fourth rising sun—she had passed through the forests—swam the rivers, and, all bleeding and worn out, was seen hovering round the little cottage in which her babes were sleeping!

She was seized once more;—and before her wounds were healed, she was again torn from her children, and sent away to the missions on the upper Oroonoko River—where she drooped, and shortly died, refusing all kinds of nourishment—died of a broken heart at being torn from her children! Such is the history of *"The Mother's Rock!"*

Perhaps I might make use of this touching story to lead you to contemplate the curse of slavery; or to show you how far cruelty may fill the hearts of those who profess to bear the image of Jesus Christ: but I have a different object in view, and I mention it solely to illustrate one single point, viz.—the strength of a mother's love for her children;—a feeling as universal as man, and a stream so deep, that nothing but the eye of the omniscient One can see its bottom! For, wherever you find woman, whether exalted to her place by the gospel, reduced to a mere animal by Mahomet, or sunk still lower by heathenism, you find this same unquenchable love for her children. She will cheerfully wear herself out, and go down to the grave, to alleviate the sufferings of a single child. I have now in my mind a poor widow, who told me, at the funeral of a son, whose intellect and reason had been destroyed by fits, that for *thirty-eight years* she had never passed a single night, in which she did not rise once or more, and go and minister to the wants of that child! She was literally worn out, and in a few weeks followed her son to the grave.

The heart of the mother can never grow cold. Her offspring may go out one by one, and be scattered to the four quarters of the globe; but the rivers that run, and the mountains that rear their heads, and the long deserts that lie between her and them, neither lessen her love, nor loosen the bonds which hold them to her heart. Time and distance do nothing towards extinguishing those eternal fires which burn in her heart. From the moment that she first gazes on the face of her babe, to that in which she closes her eyes in the slumbers of death, she never remits her care, her anxieties, or her love for him.

But you will ask,—Is this so without exception? Have we not read of Jewish mothers who would go out to the fires of Moloch, and with their own hand, take their babes, and dash them upon the iron spikes in the midst of the flames, and there stand and see them writhing in death, while the drums are beating all around them to drown their cries? Yes, you have read of this, and probably thousands of Jewish mothers have done it. And have we not read in the letters of Ward, (now we trust resting in heaven,) of the mothers in India at the present day, who take their firstborn, when the child is two or three years old, to the river's side, and encourage it to enter the stream till the current carries it out— and there stand and see it struggle, as it screams, and stretches its hands to her, and perishes? And have we not read of the mothers of Sauger Island, who have been seen casting their babes off among the alligators, and watching these monsters as they quarreled for their prey, and watching too the writhing infant in the jaws of the successful animal— standing motionless while they break the bones and suck the blood of these innocents! You have read all this.

How then, say you, can I reconcile all this cruelty with what I have been saying of a mother's love? I reply, I said that a mother's love was strong and deep: I did *not* say that it is the deepest thing known on earth. No! there is one thing deeper! it is that unutterable sense of guilt and ill-desert which can overcome even a mother's love, and turn her into a tiger. These awful cases only prove what I have been saying: for when the wounded conscience, knowing of no Redeemer from sin, would try to purchase her salvation, she offers the highest price of which she can conceive—the life of her own child! Oh! if we need no atonement by the blood of the Lamb, how is it that the soul, so torn that its very holiest and deepest affections are tortured away and destroyed, is ever to find peace, and confidence, and joy? What, but a Savior's blood, can pacify a conscience which will make a mother a monster in hopes of finding relief from its awful lashings!

The love which the father, the brother, or the sister bears, seems to be secondary, and the result of habit and association. But that which glows early and late, that which never tires or decays in the bosom of the mother, seems innate—a part of her very being. In such cases as that presented to Solomon, it speaks out in nature's own voice.

Now, why has God planted this *deep*, this *unquenchable, irrepressible* love for her offspring, in the mother's heart? Does he do any thing in vain? Did he ever rear a mountain, or hollow out the basin for the great waters, or even leave the impression of his hand any where in nature—much more on the human heart—unless that hand was guided by infinite wisdom? No,—he had a design in all this, and a design worthy of himself. All do not see it,—all do not feel it. The Indian mother who hangs her infant to the bough of the tree, and sings her wood song while the winds rock it,—thinks no further than to rear up her child to be a warrior, or a hunter;—the African mother who carries her infant on her back to her daily toil, may think no further than that he may be a slave under a kind master; and many a mother claiming high intelligence and refinement, thinks no further than to rear up her child to share and enjoy wealth, pleasures, notice, and distinctions. With what pride does she gaze upon her little daughter, hoping she shall yet see her excite the admiration of the bright circle! How will her heart dote, when that infant boy shall stand the first in the university, the first in his profession, and among the first in the nation! As such mothers bend over their children in all the tenderness of maternal love and solicitude, they have no conception of the design of God in creating that feeling which looks down into the future, and lives in posterity. May we not fear there are too many who profess to be Christians, who, day by day, go no further in their views than merely to train up their children for earth? I do hope there are none of this description who will read these pages; but if there are not, my readers will be very few, or very uncommon indeed.

What are correct views on this subject? Why is a love so deep, planted in the bosom of the mother, that no language can describe it? You have seen the child die, and heard the lamentations of the father. The wailings of David over his son still ring in our ears; but the sorrows of the bereaved mother are too deep for wailing. You never hear *her* voice on such an occasion. Nature has given her no means by which to convey the agony of her sorrows! Why has God created this love in her heart?

I will try to tell you. It is because he commits to her first, constant, and immediate keeping, a treasure too important to be entrusted to a love that can be measured! When he gives to the mother a child, what does he do? He has made a new creation;—he has created a *mind*, which is to think, and feel, to live, grow, and expand—for ever!—a *mind*, which is to act on other minds, and influence their destiny for eternity,—a *mind*, which is to be a vessel into which blessings or woes are to be poured,—and from which blessings or woes are to flow upon other minds for ever! A new spirit is placed under the care of that mother, which is surely to track its way in the eternal world, and in its train carry joy or misery—not for a day, or an age, or while a world lasts, but while ten thousand worlds fall away into nothing, and then it is only in the dawn of its being. Who would think it a small charge, were a young sun committed to her charge, which would shine as our sun does, and give light, and warmth, and heat, and uncounted blessings, if properly reared; but which, if *not* properly reared, would be a curse for ever to hang up in the heavens, pouring woe and death upon the generations of the earth! But know ye, that yonder infant in the cradle is a spirit which will live when that sun has done shining, and will be felt in the universe ages after his light is extinguished—will be a greater blessing than the brightest sun that ever shone, or a heavier curse than the sun would be, if every ray of his light were a poisoned arrow.

This is the reason why so deep a love is centered in the bosom of her to whom this immortal spirit is first committed. It would not do to trust it to the cool calculations of one who could stop to measure her affection;—no!—such a spirit must first be placed in the hands of one whose love is too deep for measurement.

Here, then, I take my stand; and here I feel the real dignity of the mother to begin—for God hath committed to her hands the keeping and the molding of a spirit which may for ever rise up in glory and in light. Never, this side of eternity, will the influence of the mother of Moses be known—who so trained up a child, and so implanted religious impressions upon his soul, that a kingdom and a crown could not tempt him from the service of God—the great end for which he was created! You say that you cannot expect your child to become a Moses. True— nor did she expect this. But when you see a little boy walking the street, who dare say that he may not become a man, and become a blessing in his day and generation? Recollect that our whole existence on earth is but a childhood; the manhood of the soul is in the next world, where the spirit of that child, redeemed and glorified, shall shine as the sun in the firmament for ever and ever, and shall scatter blessings as widely. Oh! if my little child is to do all that he ever does for his God, in this life, my heart would sink at the probability of his doing little or nothing; but when I recollect that heaven may be his home,—infinitude the space in which he may move, and everlasting ages the period in which he may act, with a nature unwearied day or night, who can tell the greatness of the destiny of such a spirit, or the work of rearing it up for God! Blessed be his name, he hath created in the mother's heart a love that can receive such a charge, and looking to him for assistance, can train up that child; and through patience and tears and prayers, will at last see it rise up and become "a star of day."

"We cannot," said a mother to me as she held her infant in her arms, "we cannot go to Congress; we cannot stand in the pulpit; we cannot be known, we must toil at home!"

"Cannot go to Congress!" Aye,—but if God had planted the same deep love of her country in woman's heart, that he has for her child, he would have committed to her hands the petty interests of politics and of time; but no—he has committed to her hands the future destiny of nations and of empires—all that we hold dear on earth, and what is more, the interests of the soul when time shall be no more. Oh, mother! do not mourn over your lot—that the distinctions of earth are not yours,—that the honors of men are not yours—you have interests committed to your hands too sacred to be polluted by being mingled with the honors of this world. Do not grieve in secret, at times, that the inscrutable wisdom of God has assigned you an inferior station, made your will subject to that of another, and made your glory to consist in bowing in meekness while you drink the bitterest cup which humanity knows,—your children will bless and honour you more and more as they leave your roof, till they gather round your grave as the most sacred spot on earth, and God will reward you most abundantly. He will remember the sorrows which your heart could tell to none but him.

The mother of Timothy Dwight did not know that she was rearing up a son who should be the direct means of instructing between two and three thousand pupils,—of forming some of the brightest stars that have shed their light on this land, and of producing writings which shall continue to form and mould the character of men for generations yet to come.[1]

---

[1] Solid Ground recently brought back into print Timothy Dwight's greatest written work, *Theology Explained and Defended* in four volumes.

Oh! if the fire on our altars ever goes out,—if ever another Jeremiah shall sing the funeral notes over our nation's grave, it will be because the mothers of this land have forgotten their duties and their power, and have ceased to baptize their offspring with prayer. In their unobtrusive and silent sphere of action they may be sustained by the peculiar and lofty consciousness, that in communicating the eternal principles of truth to minds created for immortality, they are doing what can never cease to be felt; and when the kingdoms and empires of earth have melted away and are forgotten, when the eloquence and wisdom of senators, with the courage of warriors, shall have passed away, their labours will be known, and acknowledged, and eternally be seen to be unfolding in new and glorious results.

The great object before the mother, then, is to train up her child for eternity—for the service and presence of God to everlasting ages.

If this be the scale on which you measure, you have something that will sustain you at all times, and on all occasions. Do you watch your infant daughter, and wish her to become *beautiful?* Think again. Of how much consequence is it, whether her dress at school for a single day be beautiful or otherwise? Is it any? And is not the body the dress of the soul, to be worn but a day?

You wish your boy to be *wealthy.* Suppose him to be on a journey among strangers, of what consequence is it whether he travel as a poor man's son, or a rich man's? The journey of life will soon be over, and he will never be asked whether he were rich or poor.

Do you wish your child to become honoured among men? And is it of any great consequence whether, as he passes through the streets, he have the applause of beggars and of the vile, if all the good in the land will honour him? Let your child have heaven honour him—the redeemed church, and angels, and Christ, and God the Father, and of what consequence are the honors of earth?

But you wish your son to do good! He will;—he will become a Newton, an Edwards, or a Brainerd, if God sees best, and if God needs his services here; but even if he does not see fit to use him as an instrument of great good here on earth, train him up for the skies, and he will he used as a glorious instrument of promoting his honour hereafter. You may not rear up an apostle here, but you may rear up an angel hereafter. You may not see him the object of admiration here, but hereafter you may see him stand among the sons of light at the right hand of Jesus!

And now the question is, *How can the mother do this?*

I will endeavour briefly to answer this question, and also a second, viz. *Why she should try to do this?*

1. *How can the mother train up her child for God?*

I reply, she must be a woman of prayer,—of daily, fervent, habitual prayer,—and for these reasons;

(a.) *She needs wisdom.*

The child must receive its first impressions and thoughts from its mother. She needs wisdom when and what and how to teach it this or that. She wants to know how to reach the mind, how to impress it, how to guide it, how to discipline it. We call this kind of wisdom *skill*; but it does not come of itself. Nor is it inherent. But it follows in answer to prayer, for God only can impart that wisdom; and the mother who does not seek it of him, may be sure she will never have it. She will not be led to say just the right things, in just the right time and manner.

(b.) *The mother, of all other things, needs self-discipline.*

Without this, how can she forego the pleasures within her reach, if she leave her child in other hands, and free herself from the responsibility? How can she watch over her child day and night, in sickness and in health, with a patience that never tires, and with a vigilance that never, for a moment, slumbers? The trials which press upon a mother are constant, un-remitted, and, except by prayer, unalleviated. Who can at all times, and under all circumstances, command her own temper and feelings, subdue and discipline her own heart, unless the grace of God help to subdue and discipline that heart? Oh! mother—you may not chide in anger,—you may not speak with impatience,—you may not rebuke with angry severity,—you may not correct in passion! Your patience must never tire, your passions must never rise,—self-comm90and must never for a moment even seem to be relaxed,—self-control must never even falter! This severe self-discipline you can seek and find only in prayer. Nothing else can give it, nothing else can retain it when given.

(c.) *The mother must be decided.*

It is not difficult to be decided, were this all: but to be decided and firm while the feelings and the voice are as soft as the notes of the lute, is difficult. Your child has no judgment. Hundreds of times every week, and many times every day, he must be denied, and have his wishes and his will submit to yours. When he is well, you must, of necessity, be constantly thwarting his inclinations, forbidding him, or commanding him; and when he is sick, you must force him, and stand further than ever aloof from indulgence. Even when you feel that he is on the bed of death, you must control him, govern him, command him, and see that he obeys! Your own decision, energy, and firmness, must never waver for a moment in his presence. While a mother's heart pleads for indulgence, you must have a resolution which will lead you to do your duty, even while the heart bleeds, and the eyes weep. That noble mother—who held her child while its leg was amputated, and did it with a firmness that he dared not resist, and with a tenderness that made him feel that she did it for his good—who does not admire? These two qualities, decision and mildness, are seldom found in man. He is either too stern, or too lenient. But the mother! she can possess them both, and have them both in exercise at the same moment. But she must have the aid of Heaven. She must seek it in prayer, at the foot of the throne, and there she *will* find it.

I could point you to a son who cherishes the memory of his mother as something inexpressibly dear and sacred. She was a widow, and he her only son. When a young man, he said something or did something in the presence of his sister and a cousin, both young ladies, highly improper. His mother told him of his fault mildly and kindly, and requested him to make an apology to the girls. This he declined. She insisted upon it, and even laid her commands. He refused. She next requested him to go with her into his chamber in the third story. He complied. She then very coolly took the key, and told him she should lock the door, and he would neither see her face, nor receive food, till he submitted. The next day she called at the door of the prisoner, "My son, are you ready to comply with my request?" "No, mother." The second day, the same question was asked and the same answer received. The third day, she went to the door, and says, "James, you think by holding out thus, your mother will yield, and come to your terms: but you do not know her. I am in the path of duty, and I shall not yield till the timbers of this house decay and fall, should I live so long!" That evening he would have sent a message to his mother, but had no messenger. On the fourth day he promised to do whatever she required. She opened the door, and her pale, sickly-looking boy embraced her with tears, asked her pardon, and submitted to her requisition. He has since been seen to shed tears of gratitude over that decision and faithfulness, and to assert with the utmost confidence, that it was this firmness in his widowed mother that saved him from irrevocable ruin.

(d.) *She needs perseverance.*

The trials of a mother are constant, unknown, and indescribably great. One of the warriors of the age tells us that in the evening after a most awful battle, he went out on the field among the dying and the dead; but nothing affected him so much as to find an officer slain, and his faithful dog lying at his breast, under his cloak, and howling in his agony. This has been admired as a beautiful picture of faithful attachment; but it is nothing in comparison with what the eye of God daily witnesses, as it looks down into the family circle, and notices the thousands of mothers hanging over their dying children.

The duties of the mother begin in the morning; they end not with the day; they incessantly call upon her till she reaches the grave. Others may have a respite; others may for a time throw off care, and anxiety, and responsibility. But the mother can never do so. She must be unwearied and faithful when no eye sees her to applaud; must sow her seed when she sees no immediate prospect of a harvest; must expect no return and no reward for her labours for years, and, it may be, for life. She can adopt no theory which is not to be reduced to immediate and constant practice. How can she have this faith, and this perseverance, unless she be in the *habit* of communion with God? The Bible and prayer must be her strength and her weapons. With these, she can carry her babes through the deserts where fiery serpents beset her path, and they shall not be bitten. Without these, she has all the sorrows, anxieties, and griefs of a mother, without any thing of those consolations which God bestows in answer to prayer. Do you wish a wisdom that is profitable to direct,—a patience that never forsakes you,—a firmness that never leaves you,—a faith that always bears you upward and onward, looking for your rewards hereafter—you *must* seek these by prayer. Without this, you can neither govern yourself, nor your child, nor persevere.

The child will receive *impressions* from the daily and hourly example of his mother, which will do more to form his character, than any and all the instructions which you may give him. The example before his eyes, will, for several of the first years of his life, be his education. Now there are certain *impressions* which you should be very careful not to make upon your child, if you would train him up on the great scale of spending eternal ages in the service of God.

Be careful and not lead your child to feel that the body is the great object for which he lives.

The first impressions which the child necessarily receives, will be, that his mother considers the body an object of great concern and importance. The great business of intercourse between the child and the mother for a number of years, is to minister to the wants of the body— its food, its cleanliness, its dress. How little does he understand that this body is only the house for the spirit to dwell in, and that, in comparison with the soul, it is of no worth! When you teach your child, when you pray with him, be careful and make the right impression as to the comparative worth of the soul and the body. Every child is naturally a sensualist. He would live to gratify the appetites of the body; and the mother, unless she looks well to this subject, and exercises very great care, will make the same impression. I have known many children who, from some defect in their education in this respect, felt that the highest of all gratifications is that of indulging in certain articles of luxury.

A second impression to be avoided is, *that you do not lead your child to feel that any earthly distinction is, of itself, of any value.*

How is it that the child so early learns that his father is a great man, and therefore he must be caressed and treated with deference; or that his father is a rich man, and therefore he may take airs to himself accordingly; or that his father has a house, or a store, or a farm, different and better than others? Who made these impressions on the child? He received them at *home*—and there estimated their worth, by seeing what value his parents placed upon them; and he values them, and is vain of them, just as example has taught him to be. The objection is not that he knows these things to be yours, but that a deeper impression is not made; viz.—that nothing on earth is of any value, except as a means with which to honour God. Let him see by your constant example and conversation that *you* feel that nothing but piety, or what may be made to promote piety on earth, is worth naming. The fashion of this world passeth away; the pomp and magnificence of life, the glitter of wealth, and the artificial splendors of time, will soon be gone, and the one great question on which the destiny of the soul for eternity balances, is, Have you served God in your day and generation?

A third impression to be avoided is, *that you do not let your child see that you have two characters.*

It requires no great art to teach a child to be a hypocrite. Let him see his mother impatient, irritable, morose when nobody but the family are present, and then see her face dressed in smiles when company are present, and she has taught him a lesson which he will never forget. He unconsciously draws the inference, that if a mild and pleasant character may be assumed whenever his mother chooses to assume it, so may a religious character; and the impression upon him is, that *all* your character is artificial, except your poor, everyday character. The next consequence is, that your religious instructions are mostly lost. Let your patience be exhausted, and your spirit be fretful and impatient as you put your weary child to bed at night, and the next moment call upon him to join you in acts of devotion, and he knows, without the power of reasoning, that such religion can have but a slight hold on the heart. Above all things, do not so live that your child shall feel that *all* your character is artificial, except the poorest part of that character; for this will not only teach him to be a hypocrite, but will shortly give him the heart of a little infidel.

One more caution. If you would train up your child for usefulness among men, and for the glory of the skies hereafter, you must *have no views which are measured by a scale narrower or shorter than that of eternity.*

It is a universal law in the moral, as well as in the natural world, that the water can never rise higher than its fountain. He who feels that it is enough for him to move in a very narrow circle will not be likely to fill one that is very wide, or to have his influence extensively felt. Just as the Indian boy, who has been taught that it is enough, if he be able to manage a canoe, will never be likely to be fitted to take command of a ship. And the mother who feels that the great object for which she lives, and for which her child is to live, is to have its body fed and clothed and sheltered, and to have him a creature of this world, will never so train him up that the immortal spirit will be likely to make eternity the great object for which he lives. But what would you think of a teacher who should take your children, and whose highest aim was to prepare them for a single half-day's exhibition during the year? This single exhibition constitutes, in his view, the whole and the great object of education! Would he be the man to educate your child? You say, No! But the little exhibition which a mortal can make here, is not an hour, compared with that eternity which is before him. What though your child appeared admirably at the exhibition, and drew many eyes upon him, yet if wholly unfitted for the trials, the business, and the duties of life, you have paid too dear for the exhibition;—and though your child may walk upon the high places of the earth, or even wear so dazzling a thing as a crown, it is but the bubble of a moment. The *day* of the soul's existence is yet to come—a day, remember, to be spent according to its training and character formed here.

I now hasten to the last question proposed,—

2. *Why should the mother do all this?*

The burden imposed upon the mother, if I am correct, is immense; and who hath required this at her hand? I reply, there are three special reasons, why she should cheerfully take all this trouble and faithfulness upon herself.

(a.) *It will hasten the salvation of the earth.*

Who has not reviewed the few past years with fear—and who can look forward without forebodings? Can you look at this age, and see the great mass of mind moved, agitated, and troubled, without fearing that shortly the agonized cry of nations, forsaken by God, will rend the heavens? The foundation of society already shakes, and nothing but the raising up of generations, who, from their very cradles, shall have the fear of God planted in their hearts, can anchor this, or any other nation, so that there shall not be a shipwreck of hopes. Arms cannot do it; wise men cannot do it; nothing but Christian principles, planted in early life, can do it. No,—paper constitutions, and printed laws, and learned judges, are all a mockery, under a free government, unless the mothers in the land do the work before their children leave their fireside.

We want *self-governing men*, for they only can do that work, without which the earth must continue to groan in bondage. Political institutions and literary institutions are of no avail. Standing armies are straw, when arrayed against the excited passions of a free people. The republics of South America have been fields of blood, scenes of anarchy and despotism—a burlesque upon the name of republics; and the reason is, they have no religion there. The brute force of arms cannot now hold *men*; they must govern themselves, or be slaves. But they can never govern themselves till they fear God and keep his commandments. We cannot save civil liberty even—to say nothing of giving the gospel to every creature under heaven—without men,—*men*, who were nurtured amid prayer, devoted to God, and to the salvation of men, from their infancy. We need whole generations of missionaries who shall rise up, clothed with salvation, and pour the streams of mercy, which flow from the throne of God, over all the earth.

Mothers! we want your sons to stand in these pulpits,—which we shall soon vacate. *Yours*, to be pillars in these churches;—*yours*, to go to the isles of the ocean;—*yours*, to labour and die on the burning sands of

Africa; *yours*, to carry light into the dark heart of India; and *yours*, to go to the snows of the north. Yes!—there will be, I trust, mothers who read these pages, whose sons and daughters ought to rise up for God, and cry, "Here are we, send us!" Train them up to this service—to the holy service of being agents in redeeming *mind*, immortal, imperishable *mind* from sin and Satan! Train them up for the work of plucking brands from burning, and quenching them in the blood of Jesus, and seeing them become stars in the kingdom of God! Thus you *can*, and you *will* hasten the jubilee of the earth; and though your eyes will soon close in death,—yet—from the foot of the throne above, you shall welcome those whom you and your children have led to Jesus. They shall come from the east and the west, from the north and the south, and shout "Grace, grace."

Train up your child to live and act for eternity, because,

(b.) *This will place you high among the sons of light.*

You remember that the poor widow gave her two mites, and it was more than all that the rich could do. The cup of cold water, offered to Christ, shall be rewarded.

But what are such offerings? Who can bring an offering so rich, so costly, as the mother who gives her child to the service of God? *She* makes a sacrifice which no money can purchase,—which no tongue can describe; and she shall have a reward proportionate to the gift. Oh! what streams of joy and blessedness will for ever flow into the heart of the faithful mother! Christ will own her as his mother,—and her sons and daughters as his brothers and sisters! Was she unknown on earth, and was the fire which she ever kept burning on the altar of her heart unseen by man? But her reward shall be sure—she shall enter into the joy of her Lord.

Train up your child for eternity, then, once more, because,

(c.) *This will place your child high in glory hereafter.*

In this life we can never know how many spirits of just men made perfect now reign in heaven, in consequence of the faithfulness of their mothers. Those now on earth, living by faith, and who "keep the sayings of this book," the most devoted men living, are those who have been led to Christ by a mother's love and faithfulness. You can hardly be aware how deep may be the impression which you may make on the mind of your child, even in a very few moments of time. For one, I can truly say, I have never met with any loss so great, as that of losing the care and instructions of my mother during my childhood, in consequence of her having lost her reason. But I can recollect that when a very little child, I was standing at the open window, at the close of a lovely summer's day.

The large red sun was just sinking away behind the western hills; the sky was gold and purple commingled;—the winds were sleeping, and a soft, solemn stillness seemed to hang over the earth. I was watching the sun as he sent his yellow rays through the trees, and felt a kind of awe, though I knew not wherefore. Just then my mother came to me. She was raving with frenzy,—for reason had long since left its throne—and her, a victim of madness. She came up to me, wild with insanity. I pointed to the glorious sun in the west,—and in a moment she was calm! She took my little hands within hers, and told me that "the great God made the sun, the stars, the world—every thing;—that he it was who made her little boy, and gave him an immortal spirit; that yonder sun, and the green fields, and the world itself, will one day be burned up; but that the spirit of her child will then be alive—for *he* must live when heaven and earth are gone; that he must pray to the great God, and love and serve him for ever!"

She let go my hands,—madness returned,—she hurried away. I stood with my eyes filled with tears, and my little bosom heaving with emotions which I could not have described; but I can never forget the impressions which that conversation of my poor mother left upon me! Oh! what a blessing would it have been, had the Inscrutable providence of God given me a mother who could have repeated these instructions, accompanied by her prayers, through all the days of my childhood! But—"even so, Father, for so it seemeth good in thy sight!"

There is a gift which the mother can bestow—the richest in the universe of God. She cannot give her child earthly distinctions;—she cannot say that earthly blessings shall be his,—but she can do more;—she can place a crown of life upon his head, and see him shine forth in the kingdom of God, as the sun in the firmament, for ever and ever!

Mothers! if when the sorrows of life shall be over, when the fashions of this world shall have passed away—when the sea shall be dried up,—if you may stand on Mount Zion above, with your children around you, able to say, "Here, Father, am I, and here are the children which thou hast given me,—of those whom thou gavest to me have I lost none," [*cf.* John 18:9] and shall hear him say, "Well done, good and faithful servant, thou hast been faithful" [Matt 25:23]—would you exchange that hour for all that ever entered into the heart of man? Take these children, then, and train them up for God, and all this, and a thousand-fold more, shall be yours for ever!

Will my reader permit me before we part to ask her to go with me to yonder chamber.

The house is still,—the curtains are drawn,—the world is shut out, and they are waiting for the dark messenger.

Who is that pale one on the couch of death, calmly breathing her soul out in prayer? The eye of faith is bright, clear, steady. Hope spreads her wings,—the house of clay shakes, and the spirit is preparing to mount upwards.

Who are those who stand around the bed, weeping and yet rejoicing? Do you not know them? That son is a minister of the gospel, and has come to catch the mantle of his dying mother. That other son is a devoted, distinguished member of Christ's kingdom; and these daughters are all polished stones in the living temple of God. She has committed them to God; and she has prayed for those other children, who are laboring for Christ, far away among the heathen. This was a faithful mother. She trained her children up for God.

She has now done with prayer; the song of praise begins, and she hears her Saviour call, "Come up hither!" The eye closes, the heart is still,—and the spirit goes "straight up!" And who is that angel, and that cherub, who meet her ransomed spirit, and lead it to the Lamb? These are those children whom she laid in the grave years ago, amid many tears! She now reaches the throne,—sees the Redeemer, and now the sweet song of love breaks from her lips,—"*My soul doth magnify the Lord, and my spirit hath rejoiced in God my Saviour! For he hath regarded the low estate of his handmaiden; for behold, from henceforth all generations shall call me blessed. For he that is mighty hath done to me great things, and holy is his name. And his mercy is on them that fear him from generation to generation.*"

Come back now to earth, and leave what we cannot comprehend. Let her generation pass away; let all generations of men rise up and pass away like shadows; let the earth itself flee away,—the heavens and the universe, all depart. Let ages, ten thousand times ten thousand ages, pass away, and once more let us go and look in upon that bright multitude! Do you see that burning seraph,—the spirit that hangs upon the Redeemer's looks,—the spirit that glows and pours out the song so loud, so sweet, so unceasing? It is the same spirit, who, ages before, laid the foundation for all this, by being a faithful mother while on earth! Her rewards are ever fresh from the hand of the Saviour, and to eternity they unceasingly increase.

Mothers! if in this short interview I have said any thing that will meet the approbation of Christ, I believe it will do you good; if any thing contrary to his will, I pray that it may be pardoned. If what I have said shall quicken one of you in duty, lead you to one degree more of faithfulness, I shall feel that I have not addressed you in vain.

In the volume, and perhaps volumes, which follow, I have endeavoured to aid you in the great work of training up your child for God, by aiding you to teach him the great truths of revealed religion. A more difficult work could not well be undertaken; but I hope it is so written that you will approve of it; and when *He*, who is the believer's life, shall appear to make up his jewels, I hope that we and our dear children shall rejoice together.

CHARACTER OF GOD

LECTURE 1.—IS THERE ANY GOD?

EVEN A CHILD IS KNOWN BY HIS DOINGS.—Prov 20:11

Can a child reason?—Bolted door—New book—The text—Family visit—Dead brother—How to know about him—Pond—Bridge—Mill—Boat—Yard—Garden—Room—Sisters' treasures—Father's care—Application of the story—How we know about God—Two hard words used—Explained—Boy's hammer—Girl's doll—Greenlander reasoning—His kayak—The shipwreck—Marks on the sand—Reasoning—Barn on fire—The universe—What is chance?—Its folly described—Story of man cast away—His island—Sees something—Description of it—Reasoning about it—A dialogue about it—Conclusion of the story—Beautiful house—Steps—Windows—Walls—Paintings—Not done by chance—Homer—His poems—Arabs' stories—City in the desert—Curious story of Columbus—Heap of watches—Heathen can know about God—Four remarks—First remark—Second remark—Third remark—Last remark.

THE SEQUEL

Letter to Mr. Todd—The answer.
The curious dream—Hafed—His beautiful home—His family—White Peacock—Death of his wife—Death of his children—His wicked wish—His garden—A new world—Inhabitant—Dialogue—Description of the chance world—A chance man—His eyes—A chance sister—A young lady—Her features—A chance duel—A chance wound—Chance cattle—A chance herd—The happy owner—A chance sun—Measuring time—A misfortune—A house in the chance world—A chance feast—Effects of heat—Hafed's reflections—Hafed awakes—His views altered—Conclusion—*Spectamur agendo*—Lines on hearing this Lecture.

Can a child reason? I do not ask if he can reason as well as a learned man or a judge; I know he cannot, any more than he can lift as much as a strong man. No little boy here can take a book and lift it up as high as a tall man,—but he can lift it up as far as he *can* reach, just as well as the tallest man in the world. Just so a child can reason, as far as his mind understands, as well as the wisest man living. Can I not make this plain? Suppose one of these boys should go to his bed tonight, and before he knelt down in prayer, should bolt his door. He says his evening prayer to God alone. He then places the lamp on the table and goes to rest. In the morning he finds a beautiful new book, with his name written in it, on his table by the side of the lamp. He now looks to see if the bolt is drawn back. He finds it is. Did *he* draw it back last night after he had prayed? He tries to recollect, but cannot. Was the book there when he went to bed? No: he remembers there was nothing on the table but the lamp, and he remembers it because he thought that nothing could be set on fire by the lamp. He now *reasons* about it, and concludes, that as the book was not there when he went to bed, and as somebody must have put it there, and as no one could get in if he *had* left the door bolted, therefore, he himself must have drawn the bolt back, though he has forgotten doing it. This is reasoning.

Now, *every* child can reason in this way, and I wish all these children to keep this in mind, because I am going to reason, and to talk to you in such a way that you too must reason, if you would understand what I say. Try, now, to see if you cannot reason, and I will try to make it all *very* plain.

Let us now slowly read over the text.

"Even a child is known by his doings." What does this mean?

Suppose you go with your parents to visit a family who are particular friends of your parents. The two families have not met for many years, and you were never there before.

You reach the end of your journey, and find the family made up of the father, mother, and two little girls. They are all dressed in black, and tell you with tears, that they are sorrowing for an only son who has just been buried. They tell you he was a lovely boy of about fifteen years of age. Their hearts were set upon him, their hopes concerning him were high and strong; but in an hour he was cut down by death like a beautiful flower,—and is gone away for ever from this world.

You never saw this boy, you never knew him; all that you know is, that this was his home, and that his new-made grave is up on yonder green hillside. But you look around from day to day, and admire many things you see.

You go out and find a little pond full of ducks, old and young. "What a beautiful pond!" you say. "My son," says the weeping father, "planned that pond, and he got the eggs and raised those ducks. See! they are coming to have you feed them under the tree where he used to feed them!"

You pass over a pretty footbridge. "My son made that bridge," says the father.

A little further down the stream you find a dam across the brook, a waterfall, and a mimic mill all in motion, to add to the beauty of the walk.

You see a little boat moored by the side of the pond, just large enough to play upon that little basin of water.

You turn back and look into a little yard, where are all kinds of fowls.

The father comes up, and you are not surprised to hear him say, "My son did all this!"

You go into the garden, and find one corner dressed with great care and neatness. It has flowers, a grapevine, many roses in full blossom. At once you know that this was *his* corner.

You now turn back to the house, go upstairs, and there you find a little room fitted up with shelves and books. The walls are hung with drawings and maps. The little table has papers and books on it. There is a small bed, a stove for cold weather, a box for the wood, a flute on the shelf, and every thing in beautiful order. The dog lies in one corner on an old cloak, and will hardly leave the room. Do you need to have the father come and say, "This was my son's room?"

The little girls ask you to go and see their treasures. There are their small bookcases, one for each, their little tables, their stools and boxes. They tell you their brother William made them all before he died.

Can you not now, children, understand my text?—"'Even a child is known by his doings?" [Prov 20:11] Can you not now mourn with these parents who have lost such a son, and these sisters who have lost such a brother?

The mother places her feet upon the stool which *he* made for her comfort. The father walks with the cane which *he* bought out of his small purse. The animals are fed and sheltered in houses which *he* built for them. Do you wonder that this family are in deep sorrow? Have you any more doubts that such a son was living there, than if you had seen him, and seen him do all these things? Do you not begin to love him for what he has done? Certainly;—for "even a child is known by his doings," and you judge of him by what you see.

Now it is exactly in this way that we know there is a God.

We have never seen him, seen his shape, nor heard his voice; yet it is just as certain that there is a God as if we saw him every moment. Indeed, you could not see God with your eyes, for he is a spirit. When you look at a man, it is not the soul, the spirit, the *man*, which you see, but only the house,—the body in which the soul lives. The body moves, or speaks, or does something. And if God should show himself to you, it would be a body in which he dwelt, and not God himself. So that when you see what God has *done*, you are just as certain there *is* a God, as if you saw him doing the things.

But I must now use two hard words. Will you try to keep up and understand them? The two words are, *Cause* and *Effect*. But I will make them easy to be understood.

You all know that when any thing is done, somebody or something must do it. If a ball rolls on the ground, something must make it roll. If a pin drops, its weight must make it drop. If a gun goes off, there must be powder in it to make it go; and if powder burns, there must be fire to make it burn. Everybody knows this, and feels this; and this is what I mean. That which *does* anything, is the cause; and that which *is done*, is the effect. Give a very little boy a hammer, and he strikes and makes a noise. He does it a second time, and he is just as sure that the noise will follow the second blow, as an old man would be. The little girl is just as sure that somebody made her doll, as if she had seen it made; and children always ask, Who did this thing, and who did that thing?—and they know that every effect must have a cause. Now see what I am going to do with this cause and effect.

The Greenlanders are a very ignorant people. They eat seals, and whale-oil, and raw fish, and any thing, and seem almost to be men-fish. But even they know that somebody must have made all the things which they see. One of them said these very words to a missionary.

"It is true we were ignorant heathens, and knew little of God till you came. But you must not think that no Greenlander thinks about these things. A kayak, (Greenland boat,) with all its tackle and implements, cannot exist but by the labours of man. But the formation of the meanest *bird* requires more skill than the best kayak, and no man can make a bird. There is still more skill required to make a man. But by whom was he made? He proceeded from his parents, and they from their parents, and whence did *they* proceed? Common report says they grew out of the ground. If so, why do not men grow out of the ground still? And whence came the earth itself, the sun, the moon, and the stars? Certainly there must be some Being who made all these things—a Being more wise than the wisest man." So the poor ignorant Greenlander thought, and felt, and reasoned.

Just so learned men think and feel. A great ship was once dashed to pieces in a storm, on an island. There was a learned man on board by the name of Aristippus. The people of the ship all expected to be torn in pieces by wild beasts, or murdered by savages. But on the sand of the seashore, Aristippus found some rude figures drawn, or marked out,—such figures as are used in studying mathematics. "Let us take courage, my friends," he cried out in joy, "for I see the marks of civilized men!"

Now, how came he to think that *men* made these marks in the sand? Why did he not think that the winds or the waves of the sea made these marks? Why did he not think that a bird made them with his claws, or a lion with his paw? Or why not think that a savage made them with the end of his bow? Because this learned man knew that there must be some *cause* for these figures: and because they were so round, or square, or true, he knew that they must be made by some man who had been educated and taught. This is the feeling of everybody all over the world. If you were to look out of your chamber window in a dark night, and see a barn in flames, you know that *somebody* must have carried fire into it. If you travel and find a man murdered in the road, you know that somebody must be the murderer. We never see any thing done, when somebody or something did not do it. And if a man should say that he had seen a house rise up out of the ground, built by nobody, we should say, It cannot be; that man must either have lost his reason, or be a great liar.

We know that something, or somebody, must have made the sun, the moon, the stars, the world in which we live, the mountains and hills, the oceans and rivers, the trees and the flowers, the men and the animals. I say somebody or something must have made all these.

But did they not all come by *chance?*

By *chance!* And what is *chance?* I have heard some few people talk about chance, as if there were no God, and as if all things were made by chance! It is curious to know, that these people do not pretend that chance has done any thing else, except the most wonderful of all things—that of creating all things! Now lest when you grow older some wicked man may try to make you think that *chance* could do all these things, I want to talk a little about it, and make it plain to you.

Suppose I could find one of these wise-feeling men, who say there is no God, on a desert island, all alone. He was cast away in the ship and left there in a storm, when all were drowned except himself. He has built him a little house of stones and dirt; he sits at the door and looks off on the waters as far as the eye can reach, and sees nothing but the dark blue sea, and the heavens, and the sun rising up out of the waters in the morning, and again going down, yellow as gold, into the waters at evening. I say to him,

"Sir, do you see that little white spot on the face of the great waters, far off to the right hand?"

"Yes, I see it."

"Well, it is a ship. It grows as we gaze. The sails are spread, and it looks like a ship. See! the streamer hangs at the mizzenmast, the flag hangs over the tafferel, and the tapering masts shoot far up towards the sky. She bounds on from wave to wave,—fleet as the Arab's horse. She obeys the helm,—she comes up by the island, the sails drop, the anchors plunge from her bow, and she pauses and sits like a beautiful bird upon the waters. Do you see all this, sir?"

"Yes, yes, I see it all."

"What makes the tear stand in your eye, and why does your heart throb so?"

"Why, don't you see that form on the waters,—that beautiful ship?"

"Yes, I am astonished at seeing what *chance* can do! Only see there! The wood grew into the shape of that ship by *chance*. It fell into the water and floated away. The grass and weeds around the wood took the shape of ropes, shrouds, haul-yards, and also of sails. That is not a real ship, sir, it is only the work of *chance*!"

"Why," says this believer in chance, "I thought that it was a ship, and that *men* are in it, and that I should go away in it to my home, and leave this gloomy island for ever."

"Oh, no! sir, you are mistaken. There are no marks of design about that thing. It is all the work of chance. No *mind* ever planned it."

"But I see masts and shrouds, the bowsprit and the yards!"

"Yes, but it is all the work of *chance*! It grew so by *chance*!"

"But I hear music, and know those to be the tunes of my own dear country!"

"No! that is the wind whistling through the ropes, and by *chance* it strikes the ropes so as to give the sound of the drum, the fife, and the bugle; and then the wind changes a little, and another tune follows. But it is all by *chance*! Those flags, with stars and stripes on them, are all the work of chance!"

"Now, don't try to make me believe that any longer. I *know* that to be a ship, built by *men*, rigged and managed by men, just as well as if I had seen every stick of her timbers hewed, and every plank laid. There is no chance about it!"

And yet such men pretend that *men* who can build the ship;—the wood and iron of which she is built, the waters on which she sails, and the winds which move her, are all the work of *chance*! Do not even these children see how weak and foolish this is?

But suppose you go with one of these believers in chance, on some pleasant day. He tells you that he is now going to show you what *chance* can do.

You follow him upstairs, into a long and a high room. As you go up the steps, he begins to talk to you.

"Do you see these beautiful stone steps? They were all laid so by chance! No, not *laid* so, but happened to be so. This long room was made by chance. These windows *happened* so, and they are very convenient. These walls, you see, are all hung round with paintings and pictures;—no—not *hung* round,—for that means design, but the walls are covered with colors, all thrown on by chance. How beautiful! Now let me point out, and show you what wonders *chance* can do! Do you see that corner?"

"Yes," you say, "I see a beautiful likeness of Washington."

"Well, do you see that?"

"Yes, I see a picture of Bonaparte, by the side of one of George III. And along yonder I see the likeness of all the Presidents of the United States. There is a child with a fawn. There is a landscape;—there a shipwreck;—and there a harvest-field full of reapers! What a beautiful gallery of paintings! Who *did* paint all these?"

"Paint all these! Why I tell you nobody. No *mind* ever made these! They are all the work of blind chance! You know that colors *must* exist some where;—no—I do not mean *must*, but they *do* exist some where and some how, and so they *happened* by chance to take these forms, and make these pictures! Can you not believe this?"

"No, no," you say, "no human being can believe this story."

Now, how can any one ever pretend, that the *mind* of man, which could paint all these things, and that these things, which are here only copied in this room, could be made by chance?

There was a man who lived a great while ago, whose name was Homer. He wrote several long poems. We have these poems now, all printed; and to print them correctly, we must use more than nine millions of letters and characters. Each one of these nine millions must be just in its place, or there is a mistake. Now suppose you should pick up these poems in a field, far away from any house; who could believe that *chance* printed and laid that book there? No. And yet all this might be done by chance, easier than the world and all things in it could be made by chance!

The Arabs are great storytellers. They tell about beautiful cities springing up in deserts, or in the caverns of the ocean; and about palaces of gold and silver,—beautiful beyond what can be told; but they never pretend that these are made by *chance*: they say they are made by fairies, or genii, or bad spirits.

Suppose you were traveling through a desert, and all at once should come into a beautiful city, without finding a single man, woman, or child in it. You pass along the street and see a palace, a temple, a courthouse, a prison, long streets with paved sidewalks, carriages, shops, and markets, and every thing belonging to a city. Could you doubt that it was built by *somebody*? You could not say that those who reared these buildings were white or black, tall or short; but you would say that *somebody* must have marked out these streets, reared these buildings, and planned the whole city. You *could not* believe otherwise.

Shall I tell you of a curious fact?

It is said that a small *weed* was once picked up on the beach of the Azores. Nobody ever saw one like it, and nobody could tell where the weed grew. Why did they not say it grew no where, and was thrown upon the shore by chance? No, they knew it must grow some where; and as it was unknown, it must come from an unknown country; and this simple fact, it is said, first led Christopher Columbus to believe in the existence of the American world! What if *he* had thrown away common sense, and believed in chance?

Were one watch taken to pieces, and all the wheels shown to you, you would say, "It is plain that somebody must have made it;" and if all the watches in the world were gathered together into one heap, we should all say, "All these could not be made by chance! Somebody must have made them!"

It is in *this* way that the apostle Paul says, in Rom 1, the heathen are without any excuse for not knowing and obeying God: for the things which are *seen* all around us, "declare his eternal power and Godhead." [Rom 1:20]

You now see, dear children, why I believe there is a God, and why your parents believe it—because *somebody* must have made everything.

I shall now close this Lecture with *four* short remarks:

1. That as there is a God who made all things, that book which will tell all about him, must be a very interesting book. Who would not like to see the man who made the first watch, or who built the first ship, or the first steamboat? Who would not like to see a likeness of David, or of Jesus Christ? So, I doubt not, you will be interested in these Lectures which I am about to preach, about the character of God.

2. As there certainly is a God, we ought to know as much about him as possible. I want you should, therefore, carefully hear these Lectures about God, and then compare what I say with the Bible, and ask God in prayer to help you to know more and more about him.

3. As God is the greatest Being, and the greatest thing about which we *can* think, so it will help to strengthen, and stretch, and cultivate the mind, every time we think of him. The men who think much about God, are always very intelligent men.

4. That as you will find God the best Being about whom you can think, so to think much about him will make you good. People who read and think much about God, are the best people in the world.

May the great God bless you, my dear children, while you hear, or read, or think about Him, and bless me while I try to make Him known to you "by his doings." Amen.

SEQUEL TO LECTURE 1

The morning following the delivery of the above Lecture, I received from one of my little friends the following letter:

Mr. Todd—

Respected sir:—When you told us in your Lecture yesterday about God, it all seemed plain to me except one thing; and that is, I don't see why it should be so *very* impossible to have things,—*some* things, I mean, come right and be right by *chance*.

Will you please to explain this, and make it more plain to me?

  This will greatly oblige

   Your young friend,

    J. B.

In reply to my little friend J. B., I will first ask him to read *Hafed's Dream*, which is the best answer I can write for him; and then to read the lines which follow, and which were sent to me by a friend, who says they were suggested by the above Lecture.

HAFED'S DREAM.

At the foot of one of those gigantic mountains in Asia, which lift up their heads so far above the clouds that the eye of man never saw their summits, stood a beautiful cottage, facing the east. The mountain stream leaped and murmured on the north; the verdant plain, where the bright-eyed gazelle sported, lay spread out in front; the garden and the olive-yard, filled with every flower and every fruit which an oriental sun could pencil and ripen, lay on the south; while back, on the west, rose the everlasting mountain. Here were walks, and shades, and fruits, such as were found no where else. The sun shone upon no spot more luxuriant; the moonbeams struggled to enter no place more delightful; and the soft wings of the breezes of evening fanned no such abode in all the East.

The howl of the wolf was never heard here; the sly fox never came here to destroy; and here the serpent's hiss was never heard.

This cottage was the home of *Hafed*, the aged and the prosperous. He reared this cottage; he adorned this spot; and here for more than fourscore years he had lived and studied. During all this time, the sun had never forgotten to visit him daily; the harvest had never failed, the pestilence had never destroyed, and the mountain stream had never dried up. The wife of his youth still lived to cheer and bless him; and his son and daughter were such as were not to be found in all that province. No youth could rein the horse, hurl the javelin, chase the lion, or delight the social circle, like this son. No daughter of kings could be found so beautiful and perfect as was this daughter, with an eye so bright and joyous, and a form so symmetrical, as hers.

But who can insure earthly happiness? In one short week *Hafed* was stripped of all his joys.

His wife went to see a new white peacock, which it was said a neighbour, who lived a mile off in the ravine, had just brought home. She took cold, and a quick fever followed; and on her return, Hafed saw that she must die. Before two days were gone, the old man was standing at her open grave. He gazed long, and said impatiently—"Cover her,—cover the only woman that I ever loved!"

The son and the daughter both returned from the burial of their mother, fatigued and sick. The nurse gave them, as she thought, a simple medicine. In a few hours it was found to be poison. Hafed saw that they *must* die;—for the laws of nature are fixed, and poison kills. He buried them in one wide, deep grave, and it seemed as if in that grave he buried his reason and his religion. He tore his gray hair,—he cursed the light of day, and wished the moon turned into blood; and above all, he blasphemed his God, declaring that the laws which he had established were all wrong, useless, and worse than none. He wished the world were governed by chance; but as this was a hopeless wish, he wished that at his death he might go to a world where there was no God to fix unalterable laws. He arraigned the wisdom of God in his government over this world, declaring that his plans were weak, and worse than none, and that it would be far better to have no God in the universe!

In the centre of Hafed's garden stood a large beautiful palm-tree. Under it was Hafed sitting, the second evening after closing the grave over his children. The seat on which he sat had been reared by his son. On the leaf of the tree which lay before him, were some exquisite verses written by the pencil of his daughter. Before him lay the beautiful country covered with green, sprinkled here and there, as far as the eye could see, with the habitations of men, and upon this great landscape the shadows of the mighty mountains were now setting. In the east, the moon was just pushing up her modest face, and the gold of day was softening into the silver of night. While Hafed looked on all this, grief began to swell in his throat; his tongue murmured; his heart was full of hard thoughts of God, which nearly amounted to blasphemy.

As the night deepened, Hafed, as he then thought, fell asleep with a heavy heart. When he supposed he awoke, it was in a new spot. The mountain, the landscape, the home, were all gone. All was new.

As he stood wondering where he was, he saw a creature approaching him, which, at first, he mistook for a baboon; but on its coming near, he discovered that it was a creature somewhat resembling a man, but every way malformed, ill-shaped, and monstrous.

He came up and walked around Hafed as he would a superior being, exclaiming, "Beautiful, beautiful creature!"

"Shame, shame on thee!" said Hafed; "dost thou treat a stranger thus with insults? Leave off thy jests, and tell me where I am, and how I came here!"

"I do not know how you came here, but here you are in our world, which we call *chance world*, because every thing happens here by chance."

"Ah! is it so? This must be delightful! This is just the world for me. Oh! had I always lived here, my beautiful children would not have died under a foolish and inexorable law! Come, show me this world,—for I long to see it. But have ye really no God, nor any one to make laws and govern you just as he sees fit?"

"I don't know what you mean by God: we have nothing of that kind here,—nothing but chance; but go with me, and you will understand all about it."

As they proceeded, Hafed began to notice that every thing looked queer and odd. Some of the grass was green, some red, some white, some new, and some dying; some grew with the top downward; all kinds were mingled together; and on the whole, the sight was very painful. He stopped to examine an orchard: here chance had been at work. On a fine-looking apple-tree, he saw no fruit but large, coarse cucumbers. A small peach-tree was breaking down under its load of gourds. Some of the trees were growing with their tops downwards, and the roots branching out into the air. Here and there were great holes dug, by which somebody had tried to get down twenty or thirty feet, in order to get the fruit. The guide told Hafed that there was no certainty about these trees; and you could never tell what fruit a tree would happen to bear. The tree which this year bears cucumbers, may bear potatoes next year, and perhaps you would have to dig twenty feet for every potato you obtained.

They soon met another of the "chance men." His legs were very unequal in length, one had no knee, and the other no ankle. His ears were set upon his shoulders, and around his head was a thick, black bandage. He came groping his way, and Hafed at once asked him how long since he had lost his sight?

"I have not lost it," said he; "but when I was born, my eyeballs happened to be turned *in* instead of out, and the back parts being outward, are very painful in the light, and so I put on a covering."

"Well, but canst thou see any thing? Methinks thou mayst see strange things within."

"True, but the difficulty is to get any light in there. I have contrived various ways to do so,—have had it poured into my ears and nose; but all will not do. Yet I am as well off as others. My brother has one good eye on the top of his head; but he only looks directly *up* with it to the clouds; and the sun almost puts it out. He shuts it most of the time during the day; but it happens to be one of those eyes that will not stay shut, and so when he sleeps the flies trouble him badly. I have a sister who has nineteen eyes in her head; but they are a vexation. She sees eighteen things too many. Even now she can't realize that she has not nineteen fathers, and as many mothers. She goes to bed, and falls on the floor nineteen times at least before she gets in. She goes to drink, and sees nineteen cups, and knows not which is the real cup. But so it happened, and she is as well off as most in this 'chance world.' But, after all, it's a glorious world, I do assure you."

"Wonderful," said Hafed.

As they proceeded a little farther, they met a young lady.

"That young lady," said the guide, "is the greatest beauty in all these parts. All our young men are bewitched by her; and there have been no less than twenty duels on her account already. You will be amazed at seeing a being so perfect."

As they met, Hafed stared more fully than is usually considered polite among the orientals. The beauty had a face not altogether unlike a human face, excepting that the mouth was under the chin, the eyes looked separate ways, and the color of the hair was a mixture of red, light-blue, white, and yellow. One foot had the heel forward, and one arm was altogether wanting.

"Wonderful, wonderful truly," cried Hafed. "Twenty duels! But I hope they were not *all* killed, were they?"

Here the beauty began to ogle and mince in her steps most enchantingly.

"Killed!" said the guide; "you seem to know nothing about us. They all met and fought together; but as every thing goes here by chance, it is not often that we can get our powder to burn. In this case only one got his gun off at all, and that did not happen to go off till night, when he was going to bed, when it wounded his hand, which has been bleeding ever since."

"Ever since! How long ago was this? She did not look as if it could have been today."

"Oh! it was two years ago."

"Two years ago; and why don't ye seek the leech, and have the poor boy saved from bleeding to death—even though he was a fool—for more reasons than one?"

"Ah! you don't understand it. Every thing goes by chance here; and there is only a chance that a man who is wounded will ever be healed. This is one of those cases, in which he will never be healed."

"I don't understand it, truly," said Hafed.

They stopped to look at some "chance cattle" in a yard. Some had but three legs; some had the head on in the wrong part of the body; some were covered with wool, under which they were sweltering in a climate always tropical. Some were half horse and half ox. One cow had a young dwarf of a camel following her, and claiming her as his mother. Young elephants were there with the flocks of sheep; horses with claws like a lion, and geese clamping round the yard with hoofs like horses. It was all the work of chance.

"This," said the guide, "is a choice collection of cattle. You never saw the like before."

"That is true,—truth itself," cried Hafed.

"Ah! but the owner had been at almost infinite pains and expense to collect them. I don't believe there is another such collection any where in all this chance world."

"I hope not," said Hafed.

Just as they were leaving the premises, the owner came out, to admire, and show, and talk over his treasures. He wanted to gaze at Hafed; but his head happened to be near the ground between his feet, so that he had to mount up on a wall, before he could get a fair view of the stranger.

"Don't think I am a happy man," said he to Hafed, "in having so many and such perfect animals. Alas! even in this happy and perfect world, there are always drawbacks. That fine-looking cow yonder happens to give nothing but warm water for milk; and her calf, poor thing, died the first week. Some of them have good-looking eyes, but, from some defect, are stone blind. Some cannot live in the light, and few of them can hear. No two eat the same food, and it is a great labour to take care of them. I sometimes feel as if I had almost as lief be a poor man."

"I think I should rather," said Hafed.

While they were talking, in an instant, they were in midnight darkness. The sun was gone, and Hafed could not for some time see his guide.

"What *has* happened?" said he.

"Oh! nothing uncommon," said the guide. "The sun happened to go down now. There is no regular time for him to shine; but he goes and comes just as it happens, and leaves as suddenly as you see."

"As I *don't* see," said Hafed; "but I hope he will come back at an *appointed* time, at any rate."

"That, sir, will be just as it happens. Sometimes he is gone for months, and sometimes for weeks, and sometimes only for a few minutes. Just as it happens. We may not see him again for months, but perhaps he will come soon."

"But how do you talk about months, and days, when you have no such things?"

"I will soon tell you about that. We measure time here by the *yard*"—

"By the yard?"

"Yes; we call that time which the most perfect men among us take in walking a *yard*, to be the sixtieth part of an hour. These hours we reckon into days, and these days into years. To be sure, we are not very exact, because some men walk so much faster than others; but this is just as their legs happen to be long or short."

As the guide was proceeding, to the unexpressible joy of all, the sun at once broke out. The light was so sudden, that Hafed at first thought he must be struck with lightning, and actually put his hands up to his eyes, to see if they were safe. He then clapped his hands over his eyes, till he could gradually bear the light. There was a splendour about the sun which he had never before seen; and it was intolerably hot. The air seemed like a furnace.

"Ah!" said the owner of the cattle, "we must now scorch for it. My poor wool-ox must die at once! Bad luck, bad luck to us! The sun has come back much nearer than he was before. But we hope he will happen to go away again soon, and then happen to come back further off the next time."

The sun was now pouring down his heat so intensely, that they were glad to go into the house for shelter—a miserable looking place indeed. Hafed could not but compare it with his own beautiful cottage. Some timbers were rotten; for the tree was not, as it happened, the same thing in all its parts. Some of the boards happened to be like paper, and the nails tore out, and these were loose and coming off. They had to do their cooking out under the burning sun; for when the smoke once got into the house, there was no getting it out, unless it happened to go, which was not very often.

They invited Hafed to eat. On sitting down at table, he noticed that each one had a different kind of food, and that no two could eat out of the same dish. He was told that it so happened, that the food which one could eat, was poison to another, and what was agreeable to one, was nauseating to another. Selecting the food which looked most inviting, Hafed attempted to eat. What was his surprise when he found that his hands did not happen to be under the control of his will, and, instead of carrying the food to his mouth, these active servants put it into his right ear! On examining, he found it was so with all the rest, and by imitating the company, and twisting his head round over his right shoulder, and placing his mouth where the ear was, he managed to eat. In amazement, he asked how this happened.

"Ah!" said they, laughing at his ignorance of the world, "we have no fixed laws here. All is chance. Sometimes we have one or more limbs for a long time which are not under the control of our will. It is just as it happens. So when we drink, we find it always true, that

> 'Some shed it on their shoulder,
> Some shed it on their thigh;
> And he that does not hit his mouth
> Is sure to hit his eye.'"

"I suppose that to be coffee," said Hafed, "and I will thank you for a cup."

It was handed him. He had been troubled with a toothache for some hours, and how did he quail when, on filling his mouth, he found it was ice, in little pieces about as large as pigeon-shot!

"Do you call ice-water coffee here?" said Hafed, pressing his hand upon the cheek where the tooth was now dancing with pain.

"That is just as it happens. We put water over the fire, and sometimes it heats it, and sometimes it freezes it. How can it be otherwise, when we have here no fixed laws of any kind? It is all chance-work."

Hafed rose from the table in anguish of spirit. He remembered the world where he *had* lived, and all that was past. He had desired to live in a world where there was no God,—where all was governed by chance, so far as there was any thing that looked like government. Here he was, and here he must live. He threw himself on a bed, and recalled the past—the beautiful world in which he had once lived; his ingratitude, his murmurings, and his blasphemy against the wisdom and the goodness of God. He wept like infancy. He would have prayed, and even began a prayer; but then he recollected that there was no God here—nothing to direct events—nothing but chance. He shed many and bitter tears of repentance. At last he wept himself asleep.

When Hafed again awoke, he was sitting under his palm-tree in his own beautiful garden. It was morning. At the appointed moment, the glorious sun rose up in the east;—the fields were all green and fresh; the trees were all right end upwards, and covered with blossoms; the beautiful deer were bounding, in their gladness, over the lawn, and the songsters in the trees, which, in plumage and sweetness, might have vied with those that sang in Eden, were uttering their morning song.

Hafed arose,—recalled that ugly dream, and then wept for joy. Was he again in a world where chance does not reign? He looked up, and then turned to the God of heaven and earth,—the God of laws and of order. He gave glory to him, and confessed that his ways, to us unsearchable, are full of wisdom. He was a new man. Tears indeed fell at the graves of his family; but he now lived to do good to men, and to make others happy. He called a young and worthy couple, distant relatives, to fill his house. His home again smiled, and peace and contentment came back, and were his abiding guests.

Hafed would never venture to affirm whether this was a dream or a reality. On the whole, he was inclined to think it real, and that there is some where a "chance world;" but he always shook his head, and declared that, so far from wishing to live there, nothing gave him greater cause of gratitude as he daily knelt in prayer, than the fact, that he lived in a world where God ruled,—and ruled by laws fixed, wise, and merciful.

SPECTAMUR AGENDO

LINES

WRITTEN ON HEARING MR. TODD'S FIRST LECTURE

A mimic mill was on the stream;
A pond sent up its cheerful gleam;
The ducks upon the surface played;
The poultry by its margin strayed;
A windmill clattered on the shed;
The martens near their younglings fed
Or, perched upon their little roof,
Beheld their insect food aloof;
An orchard there with many a shoot,
Too young to yield its pleasant fruit;
A little rake upon the wall;
A little cart a child might haul;
A little shed, the chickens' home,
Whence from their parent they would roam;
A hive within a fragrant bower;
A well-wrought plat with many a flower:
These were the things that met the eye,
But *he* who made them was not by.

Within the house a little stool,
That showed a nicely-handled tool;
A little bedstead, and a nut
Into a basket neatly cut;
A little table and a chair:
But *he* who made them was not there.
The parents said it was their son,
Who all these various things had done;

Had built the mill, the pond had made;
Had reared the ducks that on it played;
Had made his sisters many a toy,
And built that house, the martens' joy;
Had nursed those trees and made them thrive;
Had made the bees their curious hive;
Had dug the plat and reared the flowers,
To cheer the summer's sultry hours;
Had made the cart in which might ride
His little sisters, side by side.
Their books the little sisters brought,
Their brother's hoarded pence had bought.
They showed the shelves their brother made,
With minerals and dried plants arrayed.
Within the door these lines appeared,
Doubly by William's death endeared:
"Remember Him who made the stone
To shine with colours of its own;
Who made the plant the eye to please,
And made the eye the plant that sees.
May you be gems of heavenly dye,
And plants to bloom above the sky."

Children, this youth you never saw,
But could you not his portrait draw?
Say, was he gentle, kind, and good,
Or selfish, and of surly mood?
Did useful skill his hands employ,
Or was he but an idle boy?
Think you he sought his God in prayer?
Or was *this* world his only care?
He's gone; but still in actions lives;
Then read the lesson that he gives.

Whence comes the green that clothes the fields?
And whence the food that nature yields,
Adapted to each different taste,
And in its proper region placed?
Whence comes the fur that warms the bear,
That on the icebergs makes his lair?
The fat in which the whale is rolled
To screen him from the arctic cold?

Whence comes the beauty that we see
In every flower and every tree!

Who taught the nightingale to sing,
And gave the jay his painted wing?
Who made the eye, shall He not see
The wonders he has spread for me?
Nature declares there is a Power
Around and in us every hour,
Who knows our wants, sustains our frame,
Whose kindness, every hour the same,
Calls for our gratitude and love,
Bids our affections soar above
The transient forms around us strown,
And cluster round his holy throne.

G. F. M.

LECTURE 2.—GOD A SPIRIT

GOD IS A SPIRIT.—John 4:24

———————

Hiero—The heathen philosopher—His answer—God a rock—Why?—God a tower—Hebrews want a word—*First reason why God is called a spirit*—What cannot be seen—Angel visits—God a spirit—*The second reason*—The little dead boy—His death—God not heard—*Third reason*—The lightning—The holy Daniel—China—The absent brother—*Fourth reason*—Sodom's burning—The angel in Egypt—Angel in Palestine—Awful power—God's power—*Fifth reason*—What must die—What cannot die—*Sixth reason*—Angel-students—Ignorance of a child—What angels do—What God knows—*Why God is unlike a spirit*—First reason—God had no beginning—*Second reason*—Angels have changed—A spirit learns new things—God does not—*Third reason*—A spirit limited—A spirit not in two places—Not so with God—*Fourth reason*—Spirits are servants—God not controlled—*Four things to be remembered*—*The first*—Pictures supposed—Why we make pictures—No picture like God—*Second thing to be remembered*—A good man's comfort—*Third thing to be remembered*—How God sees us—The dirty dress—*Fourth thing to be remembered*—The noblest thing—No picture of Christ—How Christ seen.

Children, did you ever hear of *Hiero,* king of Syracuse? He was a heathen; but he one day saw a learned man, and said to him,

"Tell me, what is God?"

The heathen philosopher desired *one day* to think about it, before he answered the king. This request was granted, in order to get a clear answer.

Being asked the same question the next day, he desired *two* days more to think about it; and every time he was asked, he wished the time doubled, in which he might think about it. The king was surprised, and asked why he did so.

"Because," says the poor man, "the more I think about God, the less I hope to understand him!"

This was a wonderful answer. And *we* shall find, the more we think about God, the more we shall be lost in wonder.

Why is God called a *Rock* in the Bible? Do you think it is because he is hard, or cold, like a rock? No. But he is *like* a rock in one thing—he is not *moved*, or *changed*. A little boy may climb up a great rock, and play upon it, and then go away and not see it till he is a man; but when he *does* see it, the rock is just as it used to be,—it is not *moved* or *changed*. You might sit down behind a great rock, and the strong wind might blow, and you would be safe; it would not move. You might have a cannon fired at you, and you would be safe: the rock would not move. Thus God is a rock, because he does not change, and because he makes his people safe.

You now see why God is called a *tower*, in the Bible. You might be in a strong tower, and the storm might rage around it, or armed men might try to break in and kill you,—but you would be safe. Thus because God keeps his people safe, he is said to be a tower, or like a tower.

The Hebrews had no such word as our word *like*; and so when they wanted to say that one thing is like another, they said it is the thing: thus, we should say, "The Lord is like a tower;" but they say, "The Lord is a tower." We should say, This is like my body, and like my blood, shed for the remission of sins; but as they had no such word as like, they say, "This is my body," and, "This is my blood."

Just so in my text. God is said to be a spirit: "God is a spirit;" that is, he is *like* a spirit in many things; and in many he is *unlike* a spirit. Let me make this plain.

1. *God cannot be seen, and therefore he is like a spirit.*

You can *see* many things, such as a house, a mountain, a rock, a tree, and men. They are not spirit. *They are coarse.* But the wind which tears up the great tree you cannot see. The heat which the sun pours down you cannot see. The pity which makes your friends weep, as they hang over your sick bed, you cannot see. The love which makes you think of your home and your parents, while away, you cannot see. So there are angels which you cannot see. They are spirits. They might come and watch around your bed at night; they might now be in this very house, and walking up and down these aisles to see who is listening,—but you could not see them. They see us, and are called in the Bible "a great cloud of witnesses."

But you will ask, Have not spirits been seen? Did not Abraham, and Lot, and the prophets, see angels? Yes, they did. But the angels had to come in a human body, like men, or else they could not have seen them.

Thus God is called a spirit, because we cannot see him. "No man hath seen God at any time." He is in heaven, and he is here in this house; he is with you every moment; but you cannot *see* him, because he is a spirit.

2. *God is like a spirit, because a spirit cannot be heard.*

I once attended the funeral of a little boy, two or three years old. He lay in the coffin, while his pale mother, with his twin-sister in her arms, stood over him. His light, silky hair lay parted on his white forehead. In his little hand was a small rose, just beginning to open. Could he *feel* that rose? No. Could he smell it? No. Could he hear the stifled sobs of his mother? No. Why not? The *hand* was there,—the *nose* was there,—the *ear* was there! Why could he not feel, and smell, and hear as well as ever? Because his *spirit*, the soul, the mind, was not there. It was gone away to God who made it.

Now, when that child died, there were several people in the room; but could they see or hear the spirit of the little boy, as it left them to go into eternity? Suppose angels had been there, come to carry his soul up to Jesus, could their steps have been heard? No,—you cannot *hear* a spirit as he moves.

God is such a spirit. You cannot hear him as he comes to you. You lie down at night, tired and sleepy. He comes to your bedside to watch over you, and to shut your eyelids. But you hear not his footsteps in the room. In the morning he opens your eyes, and pours the chamber full of light. But he makes no noise. He lifts up the great sun, and sheds light over all the earth, but you hear him not. He is a spirit.

3. *God is called a spirit, because a spirit is very quick in moving from one place to another.*

Did these children never look out in the dark evening, when the black clouds were rolling over head, and when the heavy thunders were near by? You have seen the quick flash of lightning. How it blazed, and showed every thing around for a moment, and then it was gone! We never saw any thing move as quick as lightning. But the Bible tells us that the angels move as quick as lightning. "Who maketh his angels spirits, and his ministers a flame of fire," Heb 1:7.

When Daniel was praying on the banks of the river, where he could be alone, even during his prayer, the angel Gabriel flew from the third heavens, and came down to the weeping prophet, Dan 9:21-22.

Just so God is said to move quick, like a spirit. "And he rode upon a cherub, and did fly: yea, he did fly upon the wings of the wind," Ps 18:10.

Do you know how far off China is? It is many thousands of miles; and you would have to sail in the ship for many weeks before you could get there. A little boy once had a brother in China; and he knew that every night at sunset this brother went up into his little room for prayer, when he prayed for his parents and his little brother at home. Now let this little boy stand in the door of his father's house, and see the sun go down. How long would it take him to send his thought away off to China, and to think of his dear brother there? It is done in an instant. Thus quick do the spirits in heaven move from one part of creation to another; and because God is everywhere, at every moment, *he* is therefore called a spirit.

4. *God is called a spirit, because a spirit has great power.*

The woman could not roll the great stone away from the grave of Christ,—but an angel could; and he could make the earth shake, and the soldiers fall down on the ground like dead men, Matt 28:2,4.

A multitude of men could not have burned up Sodom and Gomorrah in a single morning; but two angels went there one morning, and poured out fire and brimstone from the Lord out of heaven, and "lo! the smoke of them went up as the smoke of a great furnace!" Gen 19:28.

It would take an army of men to go through all the land of Egypt, and in one night kill the eldest one in every family! But a single angel passed through the land in one night, and by morning light, he had done his dreadful errand!—in every house there was crying and wailing through all the land! Exod 12:29-30.

David was a great king, and had a great army about him. A great many men could not have gone among his people, and killed seventy thousand men in three days; and yet an angel did it! Read this interesting account in 2 Sam 24:15-17.

What a great army would it take to go to another army of trained warriors, and in one night kill one hundred and eighty-four thousand soldiers! and yet one angel did all this in one night! 2 Kings 19:35. What strength must there be in such an arm! What great power has one such spirit!

What, then, must God, the Great Spirit, be? Before him the pillars of heaven tremble. All these angels are charged with folly. They are weak, they are nothing before him. "Behold, the nations are as a drop of a bucket, and are counted as the small dust of the balance," which we blow out and throw away. "Behold, he taketh up the isles as a very little thing. All nations before him are as nothing: they are counted to him less than nothing, and vanity." Oh what strength God has! And because a spirit has so much power, God is also said to be a spirit.

5. *God is called a spirit, because a spirit cannot die.*

Every living thing which we see must die. The bird that cuts the air, the fish that darts through the water, the wild beast that bounds away in his strength,—will be overtaken by death. The wisest man, and the strongest man, and the best man, must die. We go to our neighbours and help them to bury their "dead out of sight." All things around us change. New families come into the neighbourhood, the trees around become old and die. The bright sun in the heavens, the great ocean with its many wonders, and the blue sky and the stars, will all pass away, and be no more. But a *spirit* will not die. The happy angels who sang and shouted for joy when this world was created, are no nearer dying *now*, than they were *then*. God is such a spirit. "I am the Lord, I change not."

6. *God is called a spirit, because a spirit knows a great deal.*

If a bright boy should study hard, and have good teachers, and should study for a full hundred years, would he not know a great deal? But think of the spirits,—the holy angels who live in heaven. They have lived thousands of years;—they have never had to stop to sleep, to be sick, nor to rest. They have had God to teach them. Do they not know a great deal?

Besides, the angels have to do things which they could not do, unless they knew a great deal. Could a little boy go into a great ship, and be her captain, and sail round the world with her? No. Why not? Because he don't know enough. Could a poor ignorant man go and be the general of a great army, and with the army punish a nation? No. Why not? Because he doesn't know enough. Could the man who did not know a great deal be the president of a college? No. But see now what the angels do. They were sent to burn up great cities, Gen 19:28; to teach prophets and apostles; to watch over the people of God on earth, Heb 1:14; and at the day of judgment they will be sent to gather all nations before Christ to be judged, Matt 25:31. They do the errands of Christ. Now, could they do all these things unless they *knew* a great deal? Did you ever read of a mistake which an angel made? Never. Oh! if they, the mere servants of God, are so wise, and know so much, how wise must God himself be! He is a pure spirit. *He is all knowledge.* He is higher, wiser than all. No wonder the psalmist cries to the angels in heaven, "*Let them praise the name of the Lord, his name alone is excellent, his glory is above the earth and heavens.*" [Ps 148:13]

Though God is called a spirit, and in many things is *like* a spirit, yet in other things he is very *unlike* a spirit. I wish now to tell you how he is unlike a spirit in many things.

1. *God is unlike a spirit, because they were created, and had a beginning: he was uncreated, and had no beginning.*

If an angel were to come and stand in my place in this pulpit, he could tell you when the morning first opened upon this world; for he was there, and saw it. But he was then just created. He then had a beginning. But you may go back to the time when the earth was covered with waters, and darkness, and there was no creature made, and no green thing created, and there God was,—dividing the waters from the waters. Go back to the time when all was darkness, and there God was, calling for the light, and the light came. Before the mountains lifted up their high heads, before the hills were made, before *anything* was made, God was living. His life had no beginning. All other spirits borrowed their life; but he borrowed from no one.

2. *God is unlike a spirit, because he cannot change.*

A spirit was once nothing—he was not made, and by the power of God he changed from nothing into a glorious angel. The same power which made him, *could* destroy him. Not so with God. No power could destroy or change him.

Some of the angels sinned, became devils, were thrust out of heaven; they lost joy, and found woe; they stopped singing God's praises, and turned every song into curses, day and night, for ever; they no longer aid men to get to heaven, but try to ruin them. They are murderers. What a change! The bright morning star falls into eternal darkness!

Not so with God. He is the same yesterday, today, and for ever.

A spirit, too, learns new things, and thus changes his opinions. They "look into" the things which Christ is doing, and learn something every day.

They are ignorant, too, of some things. When a sinner repents, it is news to them, and they rejoice, Luke 15:10. They know not the day nor the hour when Christ will judge the world. When that day comes, they will learn many things which they did not know before. Not so with God. "All things are known unto God from the beginning."

3. *God is unlike a spirit, because he is unlimited in everything.*

A spirit must learn all he knows, as we do. God knows all things without learning.

An angel is strong, and has great power; but God can make him weak in a moment; but no one can take power away from God.

An angel may know much; he may know more than the wisest man, and perhaps more than all the wise men in the world; but he is limited: he does not know all things, as God does.

A spirit can fly swiftly like lightning; but he cannot be in heaven and on earth at the same moment. He cannot be praising the Lamb in heaven, and at the same moment be carrying Lazarus to Abraham's bosom. If an angel were here now, looking at these children, and at me, while I am speaking, he could not be in heaven at the same moment. It is not so with God. He can be here, and at the sun, and in the highest heaven, at the same moment. He hears the song of the seraphs in heaven, and the cry of the young bird asking for food, at the same moment. When you pray to God, he does not have to *come* to you,—he is already and always here, and every where.

4. *God is unlike a spirit, because nobody can control him.*

The word *angel* means *messenger*, because God sends them to do his messages and errands. The great archangel Michael is only a servant. So is Gabriel, the strong angel. They live in God, see by his light, grow wise by his teachings, and they feel that they were made to do the will of God, and be his servants. He controls them.

But who will control God? "Who hath been his counsellor? None can say unto him, What doest thou, or why doest thou thus? Behold, he putteth no trust in his servants, and his angels he chargeth with folly. He doeth his pleasure in the armies above, and in this lower world."

Now, children, there are four things about this which I wish you to remember. Will you try to do it?

1. Remember that as God is a spirit, you see why, in the second commandment, *we are told not to worship any image or picture of God.*

Suppose some one should make a man of straw, and hang it up in the room, and say that it looked just like your father! Would you like that?

Suppose you were now away off in some other part of the world among strangers, and a man should bring in a picture of a dog, or a monkey, and tell the strangers that it looked like your father at home,— would you like that? No, you would loathe it: and yet it would look more like your father than any picture or image we can make looks like God.

What poor creatures we are! If we want to make a picture of God, or of an angel, or of a devil, we make a picture of man! Why do we? Because we know not what else to make. What a foolish, as well as wicked business, is this trying to make a picture like God, who is a pure spirit! A poor, feeble, sinful man, or a beast, or bird, still lower than man, can never be copied, and make a picture which looks like God. "To whom then will ye liken me, or shall I be equal? saith the Holy One. Lift up your eyes on high, and behold who hath created these things, that bringeth out their host by number; he calleth them all by their names, by the greatness of his might, for that he is strong in power, not one faileth. Hast thou not known? Hast thou not heard, that the everlasting God, the Lord, the Creator of the ends of the earth, fainteth not, neither is weary? There is no searching of his understanding." [Isa 40:25-28]

2. *As God is a spirit, you see how he can comfort the good man.*

Two drops of water placed side by side, run together very easily, because they are alike. Two friends come together very easily, because they feel alike. And when a good man is bowed down under sorrow and trouble, God comes at once to his spirit—the two spirits easily come together—and this comforts him. Thus men may pray and hold communion with God, when the tongue does not say a word. So when a good man dies, the eye closes, the hand hangs down, the ear is deaf, but the soul can feel God present, and have peace, and joy, and blessedness. So when the body is dead and put into the grave, the soul may and does go and be with God in the world of spirits, there to commune with him for ever. The body is not necessary to enjoy God, any more than a house is necessary in order to keep a man breathing.

3. *As God is a spirit, you see how it is that you ought to worship him with a true and sincere heart.*

Children, you may stand up in prayer, and shut your eyes, and *look* as if you were praying, while your thoughts may be away at home, upon your playthings. God is a spirit, and he looks at once into the heart, and knows all about what we think and feel.

Some are hypocrites: they pretend they are good when they are not; they pretend to worship God, when they only mock him. They may deceive men, and even themselves, but they cannot deceive God. When a thought rises up in the heart, good or bad, God is there to see it.

My dear children, if your clothes were dirty and spotted, we should all see it, and you would be ashamed to come here. But when you know that God sees every spot which sin has made upon your breast, how do you feel? Do you feel ashamed of that? "To this man will I look," says God, "even to him that is poor and of a contrite spirit, and trembleth at my word. The sacrifices of God are a broken spirit: a broken and a contrite heart, O God, thou wilt not despise."

4. *You see what is the noblest part of man.*

The noblest part of man is his spirit,—that part of him which is created in the image and likeness of God. This will live, think, and feel for ever. This will not die, nor sleep in the grave. This cannot be burned up with the world. How foolish to take so much care to feed and clothe the body, and let the soul starve!

Did you ever hold up any thing before a looking-glass, and see the image in the glass? Did you ever see the impression of a seal on the sealing-wax? Well, Jesus Christ is the image of God, and the brightness of his glory, just as clear an image as the seal leaves, and just as bright an image as the glass throws back. If, then, you could see Christ, you would see God. Why then have we no pictures of Christ banded round, so that we can see just how he looked? Ah! that is not it. It is the life, the holiness, the character, the power, the mercy, the greatness, and the goodness of Christ, that are so much like God. Look into the New Testament, then, and see what Christ did, felt, taught, and what he was, and you see God. This is the only image which we may worship. Be like Christ, then, and you are like God,—are his sons and daughters, and he will be your Father for ever. Amen.

LECTURE 3.—GOD ETERNAL

I AM THE FIRST, AND I AM THE LAST.—Isa 44:6

———————

The little boy and the pond—The broken arm—Sleepless night—A long year—The old man—Going backward—What eternity is—and God—How we measure eternity—How old is God—When eternity began?—Mysteries—What we see begin—Will God stop living?—The aged visitor—Rock in the ocean—What we learn—*The first thing*—What wicked men say—Solomon's brazen sea—Day of judgment—What is before us—*The second thing learned*—Great work—What it is—*The third thing learned*—The painted boards—Furniture—Houses—Great things—World to be destroyed—Golden knife—Why the world destroyed—*The fourth thing learned*—What we need not fear—Who will remain?—*The fifth thing learned*—Why God is to be feared—His anger—Beautiful prayer.

A little boy once stood by the side of a small pond. He looked off over it, and thought it a great way across it. He looked into it, and thought it very deep; and he thought that it was a *very* great water. But when he grew up and became a man, and had passed over the great ocean several times, where he sailed many days and nights without coming to any land,—that pond seemed to be very small.

Anything seems great or small to us, according to what we measure it by.

If one of these children were to break his arm, and it became so bad that it must be cut off to save life, the surgeon must come to do it.

As you saw him take out his knives, and saws, and strings, and carefully go to work to take off the arm, it would seem a long, long time before he got through,—though it might not be more than fifteen minutes. Fifteen minutes seem a great while, when we have to measure them by great and severe pain. But when you measure them by a whole year, they seem very short.

Did you never lie down at night in health, and go to sleep, and when you awoke in the morning, have the night seem very short? But if you were shipwrecked on the great ocean, and had to hang all night by a rope, wet and cold, and expecting that the very next wave would wash you into eternity, you would feel that *one* night is a great while, and that the morning sun had forgotten to rise.

Or if you lay upon your bed, sick, full of pain, and sleepless, with friends treading softly around you, and hearing nothing but the slow ticking of the clock, oh how long would the night seem! It would seem as if the day would never return. This is because you measure the night by the pangs of pain which you feel.

A *year* seems a great while to a child; but to the old man it seems a very little time.

We think the grey-headed man who has lived seventy years an old man; but if you measure life by the lives of men who lived before the flood, what are seventy years? Measure seventy years by the whole time since the world was made, and what are they?

How old is that little boy in that front pew? Ten? Well, go back ten years, and there was no such boy. Go back fifty years, and his parents were not created. Go back over the graves of men for two thousand years, and you come to Jesus Christ. Go back, back four thousand years more, and you come to the time when this world was created. The hills, and valleys, and rivers were not made. The sun, and moon, and stars were not made. Light was not made. There was nothing. Out of this nothing the world must come:—the sun, and moon, and heavens must come. Now what can make them come? Can they come themselves? No.

But some pretend to say that there was ground and water, and wind to move the water and the dust.

Suppose there was; could dust, and water, and air, make themselves into birds, and fish, and cattle, into fields and trees, into an arm and a hand, an eye and a tongue—and above all, into the *mind* which is within us?

No! no! There are too many marks of *mind*, and we say that *mind* must have been there—away off in that dark place which we call *eternity*—before the world was made! That *mind*, so wise, so great, so contriving, so powerful, we call *God*. This is what I mean when I say, that "*God is eternal.*" "I am the first." [Isa 44:6; Isa 48:12; Rev 1:17]

A child can look into a great deep gulf, and see as far into it as a man, but he cannot see the bottom. Let me tell you what I mean by the gulf.

This world and these heavens have been made but a few thousand years; but God was living before them. What was he doing? Where was he, during that long eternity, before he created any thing which we see? Can I tell? No.—Can an angel tell? No.—Was he making other worlds, and letting millions of creatures live, and go on to the judgment?—and then was he burning up these worlds and making new ones, as he will one day burn up this world? Perhaps he was. Perhaps he did this to millions of worlds, and for millions of ages. Perhaps millions of thinking beings passed into eternity. Yes—yes—but *before* this, *before* he even made any thing,—for ages and ages before,—what was God doing?

Ah! I do not know. "Who by searching can find out God?" Who can measure an ocean which has no bottom? Who can go back, and back, and back, and say, "Here eternity began?"

Did you ever hear such a word used as *mystery*? It is a hard word, but it means something which we *believe*, but which we do not understand. Thus we believe that God is eternal, though we cannot explain what eternity is.

Some people talk as if they would not believe any thing which they cannot understand, and thus they say that they will have no *mysteries* in their religion! I do not know what such people think. If there be a God who has lived for ever, there must be about that God a greatness and an awfulness, before which the angels in heaven cover their faces with their wings. "Even from everlasting to everlasting He is God."

We see things begin. We know when that great oak on the hill was an acorn, and which perhaps was carried up the hill by a child as his plaything. We know when the oldest man was born. We know when they began to build the great city.

We know when the great sun first shed his rising beams upon the earth. But we cannot thus go back, and say, that "here God began to live." We go back till we get to the beginning of all things, and there we find God—in eternity—alone, unchanging, unsearchable, eternal!

Thus we know that God has lived for ever, because he made everything at first.

But how do we know that God may never *stop* living? Can wicked men and devils stop his living? No! no!

> "He sits on no precarious throne,
> Nor borrows leave to be."

Instead of being able to stop God from living, all men and spirits must hang on him for life.

Now, children, suppose an old man should open that middle door, and walk up the aisle—an old man, as old as Jacob—would you not feel awed before him? Why would you? Because he is so old, you say.

Suppose you were now standing at the bottom of a great mountain, and were trying to look up and see its top—away up among the clouds, where it had been hiding its head ever since the flood—would you not feel awed?

How would you feel to stand on a great rock, far off in the ocean, where the huge waves had rolled in, and dashed against it, and where the storms and the winds had beat upon it, ever since the ocean was created? What then is GOD! that great Being who has held up the ocean, and the mountain, and the world, in his hand, ever since they were made—and yet "who fainteth not, neither is weary!" He has lived for ever, and he will live for ever. A thousand years pass away, and men go down to the grave, but a thousand years are nothing to Him.

Will you not now give me your attention, while I tell you what we may learn from such a subject as this.

1. *You see how it is that the Bible says, "A day is with the Lord as a thousand years, and a thousand years as one day."* [2 Pet 3:8]

Wicked men have always been ready to cry out, "Why, the Bible cannot be true; for in that God promises to come and judge the world, but he does not come! The fathers have fallen asleep, and all things continue as they were from the beginning. How then is that promise of his coming to be kept?"

Let these men know, that God is not slack concerning his promise, as some men count slackness. He has an eternity in which to carry out his plans. He waited four thousand years before he sent his Son: and he has waited nearly two thousand years since, and yet the judgment-day does not come! Well, but what are these years to God?

You may go to the ocean and dip out a cup of water, and what is it to the ocean? You may pour it back again, and what is it to the ocean? Solomon built a great sea of brass, which would hold at least eighty hogsheads of water, 1 Chron 18:8, and you might empty all that into the ocean with your little cup of water, and what would either be to the great ocean? Compared with the *ocean*, the cup would be as the brazen sea, and the brazen sea as the cup. They are both swallowed up and are nothing, when taken out, or when put into the ocean. Just so a thousand years, measured by eternity, are no more than a day!

In this way the Bible often speaks of the Day of Judgment as just at hand. On the scale of eternal years, there is but a space between us and the judgment-day as wide as the hand, and the apostles might well say—"The day of the Lord is at hand."

There will always be an eternity forward, as great as that which is past; and, measuring by that, what are a thousand years? What is the time which this world will continue? Oh, the time will yet come, in the ages of eternity, when the whole time which the sun, and the moon, and the world lasted, will seem like a day of childhood, which the old man can just remember! Surely, in the sight of God, who lives and fills eternity, a "thousand years are as one day, and one day as a thousand years!"

2. *You see why the Bible calls this life a vapor.*

If one of these little boys had an errand to do a mile off, a day would be a great while in which to do it. If one of these men had an errand four miles off, a week would be a great while for him to do it in. But suppose a man in one year had to go across the ocean, visit England, and India, and China, and carry thousands of Bibles, and give them all away with his own hands, would not one year seem a very short time in which to do so great a work?

So it will be with you. If you feel that you live here only to eat and drink good things, and to wear good clothes, and to get money, you will have to do what many foolish, wicked people do,—contrive ways to "kill time." But if you measure this life by God's eternity, you will see that it is a vapor. You have a *great* work to do, and but little time in which to do it.

What is that *great* work? You have to learn all about God—about yourself, about sin, about Jesus Christ;—you have to repent of sin, and forsake it, to live for God, and to see how much good you can do before you go down to the grave. Time is short to the good man, because he sees that he has so much to do; and the whole life passes away like the morning vapor.

3. *You see why the Bible calls men fools, who live only to be happy in this world.*

Most men live only to be happy in this life. What would you think of a man who should get up early and sit up late, and work hard all his life long, to get a few painted boards together before he died? But what else does *he* do, who works hard all his life to get him a beautiful house to live in, and who gets it just before it is time to die? By doing so, he says,

"This house, and these painted rooms, are worth more than my life, my soul, my God!"

Some men have been known to work hard all their lives, just to get some handsome furniture in their rooms before they died. Are not these foolish men?

Some spend life in crowding and pushing, and trying to get into notice among men. They want a few honors—a little praise! But in the light of eternity what is this?

Oh, if each of these children had a mountain of silver, and a thousand men digging it out—if he had rivers flowing over sands which were pure gold—and if he had honors around his head as bright as the rainbow on the cloud, what are all these, when compared to God's eternity?

Children, you know that God is one day going to burn up this world, and all the beautiful things in it! Do you know *why* he will do so?

Suppose you had a most beautiful knife. The blade is made of pure gold, and the handle is made of precious stones—a most beautiful thing. You lay it on the table one day, and a man comes in, and snatches up that knife and stabs your mother to the heart! The blood gushes out, and she falls down at your feet dead! Tell me, now, would you ever want to see that knife again? Would you not want it put out of sight? Why? The *knife* is not to blame. True, but you don't want to see it. It is the thing which killed your dear mother, and therefore you don't wish to see it again.

So God will one day destroy this wicked world. The earth, and the sun, and the moon have not sinned, but *men* have sinned with them, and therefore God will burn them up, and put them out of sight, just as you would the knife. All shall pass away, and be burned up; and yet as far forward as you can think, eternity will be only just beginning. Is not he a foolish man who lives only to be happy in *this* life?

4. *You see how it is that good men put their trust in God.*

Those who wish to live in sin, are afraid to know all that they can know about God.

But his people!—Oh, they stand on the Rock of ages. Storms of sorrow may gather over them,—their dearest hopes may be cut off,—their most loved friends be taken away by death,—yes, the waves of sorrow may roll over them, deep calling unto deep,—and the very grave may be worn out,—the earth and the heavens depart as a scroll,—all things be seen to crumble to ruins,—still they are safe. The eternal God is their refuge, and nothing shall ever hurt them.

The golden chain which binds all holy beings together in love, is held by the hand of the eternal God. The eye that watches over all, never slumbers, never sleeps;—He foresees all things, provides for all events.

Who need be afraid of *darkness?* Everlasting light is about the throne of God. Who need fear *sorrow?* Rivers of joy flow at his right hand. Who need fear *death?* The great fountain of life and light is never to be dried up.

What a thought for a good man! His property may perish,—his body must perish in the grave,—his family melt away and be forgotten,—his name on earth perish,—the bright heavens over him, the earth on which he treads, perish,—all, all will pass away, and be no more. But there is *One* on the throne of the heavens, whose years change not,—the same yesterday, today, and for ever! He will live for ever, faithful to his promises, and faithful to bless the pure in heart, for ever.

5. *You see, once more, why the Bible says, "It is a fearful thing to fall into the hands of the living God."* [Heb 10:31]

We forget almost all our sins, but God ever lives to mark them down against us: he ever lives to remember them, and to punish them. He sits upon a throne unchangeable, holy,—"a consuming fire" to the wicked. He is the enemy of all sin,—and the wicked cannot stand in his presence.

My dear children;—you may forget God *now,* may live in sin *now,* and life may pass away, and ages may roll away, but God remains, and will punish sin.

There is no shaking off his power,—no escaping his presence,—no living beyond his years! Is it, then, a little matter, whether you and I have this God for our friend, or our enemy, during everlasting ages?

If we disobey him, he lives for ever to punish sin. Do you wonder, then, that I would persuade you to break off from your sins,—from all sin, lest he come in his wrath, "in flaming fire, with the holy angels, and punish you with everlasting destruction from the presence of the Lord, and from the glory of his power."

Let us offer this beautiful prayer together before we close.

"O Thou, who redeemedst the weak one at length,
And scourgest the strong in the pride of his strength,—
Who holdest the earth and the sea in thine hand,
And rulest Eternity's shadowy land,

To Thee let our thoughts and our offerings tend,
Of virtue the hope—and of sorrow the friend,
Let the incense of prayer still ascend to thy throne,—
Omnipotent—Glorious—Eternal, alone."

Amen.

LECTURE 4.—GOD IS EVERYWHERE

CAN ANY HIDE HIMSELF IN SECRET PLACES THAT I SHALL NOT SEE HIM? SAITH THE LORD.—Jer 23:24

A question—How know we are here—How *men* see things—How *God* sees things—*First proof*—that God is every where—Abraham—Joseph—David—Jonah—Daniel—The furnace—African desert—Sailor boy—The poor soldier—Thomas Paine—The mountaintop—*Second proof*—that God is every where—Bible proof—Clouds—Storms—Mind—Sinning heart—Young raven's cry—God in heaven—God on earth—In all parts—*Special presence*—First example—Second example—Third example—The wind, the fire, and the earthquake—Fourth example—*Awful Murder*—Mr. White—Beautiful description of it—The chamber—The blow—The deed done—*The secret*—Secret not safe—The anguish of spirit—Conscience—God in the conscience—*First thing taught by this Lecture*—The eye that sleeps not—Story of Lafayette—The *eye*—*Second thing taught*—How God sees every where—The little cabinet—*The last thing taught*—The little seed—God present in troubles—God with the poor—The orphan child—Conclusion.

Suppose on going home today it be asked you, "Who was in the pulpit?" You would at once answer the question. But suppose it be asked again, how you *know* that I was in the pulpit? You would say, Because I saw him, heard his voice, heard him say some things with which I was pleased, and some which were not so pleasant.

How do *I* know that I am present? Because I can see every part of the church, look on every face, and hear every noise.

But you see at once that I can look only at *one* place, or on *one* face, at the same moment;—that I can hear only one noise, and can think only one thought, at a time.

So I might stand on the top of the high mountain, and look off and see other mountains rising up all around me,—might see clouds rolling below me; might see rivers and lakes, cities and villages; but I could see only *one* object at a time, and if that was at a distance, I should see it very dimly and poorly.

Now this is *not* what I mean when *I* say, that *God is everywhere present, at all times, and in all places*; but I mean, that he is so present every where, that he *sees* all that *can* be seen, and *knows* all that *can* be known.

Ascend up into heaven, and God is there; lay your guilty head down in hell, and he is there; fly away on the wings of the morning light, to the end of creation, and he is there;—say to the thick darkness, Be thou a covering, and behold it will be light round about you, for there is *no place* where the workers of iniquity can hide themselves from God.

I am now going to *prove* that God is every where present, and then I am going to make the subject teach you some good things.

There are *two* proofs which I shall offer.

1. *All men, in all ages, believe that God is everywhere present.*

When Adam was in the beautiful garden of Eden, he heard God walking there in the cool of the day; and long after they had been shut out of the garden, Abel knew that God was in the places where he was, and so he built altars, and offered sacrifices to God.

Abraham heard the commands of God in his distant country, and felt that God was with him; and in all places where he wandered, he built his altars and put up his prayers.

Joseph knew that God was present when he was at home at his father's table; and he knew that he was present when he was shut up in prison far away off down in the land of Egypt.

David was a shepherd's boy,—and when he was keeping the sheep alone in the field, when he was chased on the mountains by Saul, like a hunted partridge, when he was on the bed of sickness, when he was on the field of battle, and when he was on the throne, he knew that God was present.

You have read how Jonah once thought that he could flee away from the presence of the Lord. What folly! God followed him, walking on the wings of the wind; and you soon hear the poor man calling upon

God in the belly of the fish, far down in the great waters, and he knew that God was there to hear him, Jonah 1-2.

Daniel knelt in his chamber in prayer, and felt that God was there: and when down in the den among the lions, he felt that God was *there* also, and would hear his prayer.

In Jerusalem they worshipped God: his altar was there; but when Shadrach, Meshach, and Abednego, Dan 3, were cast into the burning furnace, they felt that God was there also.

Suppose you go away from your home among strangers; do you not feel that God is there, as really as when at home by your own father's fireside? You might be travelling in the Great Desert of Africa; you might faint with hunger, and lie down alone to die. As you look around on the barren sand, you see a little sprig of green moss by your head. It is all alone, and beautiful. Do you not at once feel that God is there, taking care of that little green thing, and that he will be there to hear you pray?

The poor sailor boy has not been taught any thing about God; and yet, when he is shipwrecked, and hangs to the wreck of the vessel all night by a little rope, amid the darkness of night, and the roar of the storm, and the raging of the seas, he feels that God is there. He calls upon God in prayer, and *knows* that no darkness can shut him from the eye of God, and no roar of the storm can shut his prayer from the ear of God.

A poor soldier was found among the dying and the dead in a hospital away in a distant land, forsaken by all human beings—not a friend or relation near him; but he felt that God was there, and God would hear his prayer for his poor widowed mother, even when he was far too near death to make that prayer with words, or even to move his lips.

Men often neglect God, forsake him, and live in sin; but when they come to be in trouble, they always feel that God is present. Even Thomas Paine, on his dying bed, filthy, loathsome, and forsaken, could not help crying out, "Lord Jesus, help me." This he did often. Ah! with all his infidelity, his boasting how he was not afraid to die, and that he would live and die an infidel, he felt afraid to die,—he knew that the Lord Jesus was present, and he felt that he needed his help.

Why, if you were to go to the top of the highest mountain, where the snow and ice have hung ever since creation, you would feel that God was there. You might go into a cave so deep that not a ray of light ever entered it, and you would feel that God was there.

Oh! the time will never come, and the spot will never be found, where your soul will not feel that God is present. You will *always*, in time and in eternity, feel God to be with you.

2. *God is seen to be everywhere present by what he is always doing.*

In the spring, the herb, the grass, and the flower, awake from the sleep of the winter's grave, and the world is all clothed in green. A new generation of birds are hatched in the trees, and swarms of little fish come into life in the waters, and multitudes of insects burst their shell, and come buzzing and joyful into life. Is there not a God present to create all these? What says the Bible?

"In him we live, and move, and have our being." "Thou, even thou, art Lord alone: thou hast made heaven, the heaven of heavens with all their host, the earth, and all things that are therein, the seas, and all that is therein,—and thou preservest them all, and the host of heaven worshippeth thee." "Thy mercy, O Lord, is in the heavens, and thy faithfulness reacheth into the clouds. Thou preservest man and beast. When thou openest thy hand, they are filled with good; thou hidest thy face, they are troubled; thou takest away their breath, they die,—they return to the dust. Thou sendest forth thy spirit,—they are created: thou renewest the face of the earth."

Does the earth droop because it is dry, and the clouds drop down no rain? It is because God shutteth up the heavens, and maketh the heavens brass, and the earth iron, and the rain powder and dust, 1 Kings 18.

Do the lions come up and slay the people of Samaria? It is because God is there and sends them, 2 Kings 17:25.

Do the storms rage and the winds blow, and destroy the harvests and the houses of men? God is there, walking on the wings of the wind,—making the winds his messengers, and the lightnings his servants to destroy, whenever he sends them, Ps 18.

Does your mind grow in knowledge and understanding? It is because God is there, and "in his light we see light," and "he lighteth every man that cometh into the world," John 1:9.

Do you ever desire to obey your God, and to do your duty? He is *there*—at work at your will, "working in you both to will and to do of his good pleasure," Phil 2:13.

Do you shut out light and harden the heart? God is there to aid you, as a punishment. He "sends strong delusions that men should believe a lie." "Go, make the heart of this people fat, and make their ears heavy, and shut their eyes, lest they should see with their eyes, and hear with their ears."

Do we lie down on the bed of death? "To the Lord belongeth the issues from death,—he bringeth down to the grave."

Does the young raven cry? God is there to hear that cry, and to feed the senseless bird. Does the sparrow fly? God is there to direct the little bird where to stop for food, and where and how it shall die. Does a hair drop from your head? That mighty One who "calleth the stars by their name, and telleth *their* number," counteth the hairs of your head, and directs how and when each one shall fall.

It is easy to think and to believe that God is in yonder heavens, witnessing the flight of the great angel on the wing,—and listening to the song of the seraph before the throne,—but God's presence means more than all this:—

It means that the same God who directs the flight of the angel,—who controls the devils in their prison under chains of darkness,—who rolls the sun and the stars in their path of light,—is present to see every motion of every little fin down in the chambers of the great ocean,—to see every leap of the timid deer in the wilderness,—to hear every roar of the lion in the desert,—every cry of the bittern on the ruins of old Babylon, every pelican in the wilderness, and every shaking of the leaf in the forest, on which the insect is securely sleeping!

But there is a sense in which God is said to be present, different from all this. It is called his *special* presence. By this is meant, that in some *places*, at some *times*, God is so present, that his *holiness* is felt. For example,

1. *God is said thus to be present in heaven.*

When Israel was in the wilderness, God was with them in every part of the camp: but his cloud and his pillar of fire hung over the tabernacle, or tent, reared for him, and his *glory* hung over the mercyseat, and he was said to be present *there*, as he was present no where else.

In this sense, he is present in heaven. *There* he is seen face to face;— *there* is worshipped by his great family; *there* is seen by ten thousand times ten thousand, from every people and tongue and nation, who cease not day and night to praise him for ever. *There* he is present, as he is present no where else.

2. *God is said to be specially present in his house of worship*, like this in which we are now met.

In all other places God is present with you: but it is in his house that he has recorded his name, and he will be present to do you good. You here pray, and the prayer goes at once to his ear; you here sing his praise, and the song at once reaches him; you here sigh that you are a poor sinner, and he is at your side to hear that sigh. This makes the word of God so much like a sharp twoedged sword; and this is the reason why we seldom see a man, who has constantly been to the house of God since he was a child, live and die without being a pious man.

3. *God is specially present by the Holy Spirit.*

You know that the strong wind may blow, and even tear up the mountains; but God is not *specially* present in the wind. The fire may kindle, and burning coals go before him; but the Lord is not specially in the fire. The earthquake may shake the mountains, and crumble the rocks in pieces; but the Lord is not specially in the earthquake. Then comes "the small, still voice," [1 Kings 19:12] taking hold of the soul, making us feel that we are sinners, going to the heart and showing us our sins, and *this* is the special presence of God. It is the Holy Spirit dealing with the soul.

There is one more place where you may find the special presence of God. I mean,

4. *Your own conscience.*

Do you not know what I mean? Have you never heard something, or felt something in your heart, which told you that your soul is black with sin? Did not conscience ever show you that you are a sinner,—and then make you afraid of God, afraid of dying, and afraid of all that is beyond the grave?

I will tell you what I mean by having God in the conscience.

A few years ago, a rich and respectable old gentleman, by the name of *White*, in Salem, Mass., was found murdered in his bed. The whole town and region were moved; and for a long time, it seemed as if the murderer could not be found out. If ever murder *could* be concealed, it would seem as if *this* might be. Let me describe the awful scene in the words of a great man.

"The aged man was without an enemy in the world, in his own house, and in his own bed. Deep sleep had fallen upon the destined victim, and on all beneath his roof. A healthful old man, to whom sleep was sweet,—the first sound slumbers of the night held him in their soft but strong embrace. The assassin enters through the window, already prepared, into an unoccupied apartment. With noiseless foot he paces the lonely hall, half-lighted by the moon: he winds up the ascent of the stairs, and reaches the door of the apartment. Of this he moves the lock, by soft and continued pressure, till it turns on its hinges without noise: he enters, and beholds his victim before him."

"The room was uncommonly open to the admission of light. The face of the innocent sleeper was turned from the murderer, and the beams of the moon, resting on the grey locks of his aged temple, showed him where to strike!"

"The fatal blow is given; and the victim passes, without a struggle or a motion, from the repose of sleep to the repose of death! It is the assassin's purpose to make sure work; and he yet plies the dagger, though it was obvious that life had been destroyed by the blow of the bludgeon. He even raises the aged arm, that he may not fail in his aim at the heart, and replaces it again over the wounds of the poniard. To finish the picture, he explores the wrist for the pulse. He feels it, and ascertains that it beats no longer!"

"It is accomplished! The deed is done! He retreats, retraces his steps to the window, passes out through it as he came in, and escapes. He has done the murder!—no eye has seen him, no ear has heard him. The *secret* is his own, and it is *safe!*"

"Ah! that was a dreadful mistake! Such a secret can be safe no where! The whole creation of God has neither nook nor corner, where the guilty can bestow it and say it is safe."

Ah! there is an *eye*, which runs through all the earth, piercing through all disguises, beholding everything as in the splendours of noon—the eye of God, everywhere present!

But this is not all. God is now in the conscience of this murderer. He labours to hide his guilt deep in the heart, away from the eye of man. But oh! now begins his misery. He feels as if a serpent were gnawing at his heart, and he dares not tell God or man. He feels this serpent beating at his heart, rising up to his throat, and demanding that the secret be confessed. He thinks the whole world sees it in his face, reads it in his eyes, and almost hears its workings in the very silence of his thoughts. The heavens and the earth seem to be ready to cry out, There is blood on his soul. It rings in his ears day and night, and he can say,

> "O, it is monstrous! monstrous!
> Methought the billows spoke and told me of it;
> The winds did sing it to me; and the thunder,
> That deep and dreadful organ-pipe, pronounced
> The name of *murder!*"

The murderer may do the deed, and walk away in darkness and silence, with a "tread so softly, that the blind mole may not hear a footfall," but all will not do. His *conscience* breaks his courage, betrays his guilt, takes away his prudence; and he *must* confess the murder, or he must take his own life, and this *is* confession.

Ah! *God is in the conscience*, and he makes the worm gnaw, and the fire burn, till the soul of the sinner is in an agony. When most alone, when most hid in his own heart, and most buried in his own thoughts, God is nearest him. And there, in the conscience of the wicked, will he ever be, to awaken the worm, and to kindle the fires that shall never go out.

Now let me show you what you ought to be taught from the truth that God is everywhere present.

1. *You ought to be afraid to sin.*

We are apt to feel that God sees great, open, daylight sins, but that he does not notice *little* sins, as we call them. This is a great mistake.

You go out into the crowded street of the city, and God is there, walking the street with you. You go in, and shut the door, but you do not shut him out. You light the lamp, and he is there; you blow it out, and he is there still. You sin, it may be, in the dark, or you may sin out of the sight of man, or you sin in your own heart, or you sin by deceiving; but let me tell you that there is an *eye* upon you which never sleeps over sins,—which never winks at iniquity. Oh! if you feel that you *must* sin, that you cannot break it off, then go, go some where, where his eye cannot see you,—for *there* only are you safe! Oh! if you would but think that the great eye of God is upon you for ever, that his mighty arm is ever raised to crush you, surely you would be afraid to sin!

How dreadful is the eye of God on him who wants to sin! Do you know about *Lafayette*, that great man, who was the friend of Washington? He tells us that he was once shut up in a little room in a gloomy prison, for a great while. In the door of his little cell was a small, very small hole cut. At that hole a soldier was placed day and night to watch him. All he could see was the soldier's *eye*; but that *eye* was always there! Day and night, every moment when he looked up, he always saw that *eye*! Oh! he says it was dreadful! There was no escape, no hiding; when he lay down, and when he rose up, that *eye* was watching him! How dreadful will the eye of God be upon the sinner, as it watches him in the eternal world for ever! Who would be such a sinner? I trust and pray not any of you.

2. *You should never forget that God is everywhere present.*

When you come into the house of God, when you kneel in prayer at home, or anywhere, remember that God is there to see the heart, as well as to hear the words, and you will be more likely to worship him in spirit and in truth. In your treatment of your parents, brothers and sisters, and friends, remember that God is always present. When you *talk*, you talk in the presence of your Maker. In the sunshine, you see the brightness of God: in the heat, you feel him warming you: in the rain and the dew, it is he refreshing you: in your food, it is he strengthening you: in your sleep, it is he restoring your weary body. If you abuse yourself by eating too much, or drinking too much, or sleeping too much, he is there to see you do it. Your heart should be his temple: O do not pollute it,—do not defile it by sin.

Every creature around you, every limb of your body, every chamber of your heart, ought to be a little cabinet in which God will stay, and do you good. Enoch thus walked with God, conversing with him in spirit, asking advice when he needed it,—weeping when he felt his sins,—obeying God as his King,—loving him as his Father,—and walking and living as if God was always at his side.

3. *You see that if God is every where present, he can comfort us in trouble and in sorrow.*

The thought that God so fills heaven and earth, that he can at the same moment attend to the wants of every creature, even to the hairs of the head,—is an amazing thought! It is easy to believe that he attends to the song of the burning seraph before his throne,—that he can guide the sun and the great planets through their path in the heavens. But it is *not* easy to conceive how he can *so* be present every where, by his power and action, as to direct the motion of the small seed which the wind blows from the flower, and go with that little seed and plant it!—as to direct the little worm where to place every foot as he creeps;—as to help every little insect to open his wings and fly away;—as to be with the mite which hangs on the leaf and dies there! Yet God *does* all this—for he is every where! Oh! he does it all!

When he places you in troubles like the furnace, he is there to see that only the dross is melted away. When you go into sorrows like deep waters, he is there to see that they do not drown you. In trouble, then, be patient, and hope, for God is there to give strength, and to heal the wounds which he makes. He can turn sorrow into joy, and through thick clouds can pour sunshine and peace: he can look and show his face through deep darkness. Are you weak? He is there to give you strength. Are you a poor child, and do you need some one on whom to lean? God is always near you, and the silver and the gold, and the cattle upon a thousand hills, and the riches of eternity, are his. Are you sick, and do you love to have a physician come to your bedside? God is the great Physician who can heal both soul and body,—make your bones to rejoice, and your soul to rejoice in his salvation.

Are any of you *orphan* children, whose father or mother sleeps in the grave? Ah! God is present, a father to the fatherless, a shelter to the homeless, a refuge to the needy; and he says to you, "I will never leave nor forsake you."

Oh! children, God is here now,—seeing you all, and taking notice how you keep the Sabbath. You will now go home, to begin a new week; but do not forget that in all that you are, and do, God is with you, and his eye rests upon you.

If you will be his children, he will be with you in sorrows and troubles to deliver you;—in the hour of dying, to keep and comfort you; and in all the ages of eternity, to make you happy and blessed.

But oh! if you choose to be wicked, he will still be with you;—will go with you;—will reckon up your sins;—will write up your iniquities; and as long as your immortal soul lives, through all eternity, you can *never* go, or be,—where a holy God is not with you! Amen.

LECTURE 5.—GOD IS WISE

David—The soul wants a house—The soul's servants—The telescope—The eye more curious—How the eye keeps clean and safe—The frame of the house—The man of steel—The curious chain—The pump—Little channels—The house repaired—Witnesses against poison—The blood—The daily physician—Why we are born without dress—The elephant's head—The oyster—The muscle—The little bird—Birds wear spectacles—Little mill—Elephant's trunk—The reindeer—The whale's great coat—The clamp-fish—Food prepared every where—The ship of the desert—The soft, spongy foot—The little songster—The shark—The pilot friend—Very small watch—The insect—The strawberry-pot—Instinct—The young hen and the hawk—The beaver—How to build a dam—The bee—Infancy—Mother's love—The great basin—How rain made—The ocean a great blessing—Faces not alike—Men cannot write alike—The tongue and the ear—Day and night—The Bible—How proved from God—Jesus Christ—The wisdom of God seen—Who sees it—The world to be destroyed—New heavens hereafter—The little top—What God will do hereafter.

David looked at himself, and saw that he was wonderfully and fearfully made; and in the making of his body, he saw the skill and wisdom of God. Let me do so too.

The soul is a spirit, and it must have a house to live in. It must be not merely a house for the soul to live in, but such a house as could live in any country, and in any climate; a house that could move about whenever the soul wished to move it. What would be the best form of this house? What kind of servants shall she have, upon which she may call thousands of times every day? Let us now see.

The *feet* must carry the house about; the *hands* do whatever she wants done; the *eyes* let her know what is doing all around her; the *ear* lets her know what other minds think and feel and desire; and the *tongue* carries her wishes and feelings to other minds. The eyes are the windows through which the soul looks out; and ought not the windows to be in front, and up in the top of the house, so that the soul can see as much as possible? Where should the ear be, but near the brain, to let the soul know quickly what it hears? Where should the feet be, but under the whole house, to move it at every step?

Children, did you ever hear of a *telescope?* It is a curious thing, by which men look at the stars. It has cords, and pulleys, and wheels, and a great deal of machinery by which to turn it round, and point it any way; but after all, it is not half as wonderful as the eye. The eye has six little strings fixed to it, by which we turn it any way. If you wish to read through a telescope across this house, and then wish to look off at a great distance, you must alter it by screws, and other ways, and it is a great work to alter it. But now look at me. I stoop down as you see, and read this paper in my hand, and the next moment I look up to that further window beyond the organ in the gallery, and my eye alters itself so as to see in either place in an instant! If the eye had been *square* instead of round, would it have turned so easily as now? If there had been only *one* eye, instead of two, could it have seen as much; and if it had happened to be put out, would not the soul be left in darkness? There is a little stream of water running into the eye every moment, to keep it soft, and a hole bored through the bone of the nose, to carry off what is not used in the eye! How came that little covering over the eye, which washes it, and keeps it clean, and which defends it from harm,— which has the little skirt of fringe around it to keep out the insects while you sleep? How happens it that this little covering comes down and closes the eye when you sleep, and cannot take care of it? Do you not here see God's wisdom in this?

Let us look at this house of the soul still more. The *bones* are the frame of the house. Now there are two hundred and forty of these little timbers in your body, and every joint in the right place and of the right kind. These joints are tied together with little cords, so that every joint plays easily, and is amazingly strong. But why do not these joints wear out? Make a man of *steel*, and use his joints as much every day, and he will soon wear out. But every joint in your body is oiled and refitted every day, so that there is no wearing out. Is not all this wise?

Suppose a man could make a *chain* with twenty-four links, which could turn every way, and be so strong as to support itself upright, and hold up a great weight; would he not be a curious man? But the backbone is like this. It has twenty-four joints, turns every way, is very strong, and supports the whole body. What a wise Being was he who planned all this!

The *heart* is a kind of pump in the very middle of the house; it goes day and night, whether we are awake or asleep, and opens and shuts more than sixty times every minute of our lives. In a man, it drives twenty-five pounds of blood through every part of the body once in four minutes all his life. There are little channels running all over the body, through which the blood runs; and these little brooks are so small and so thick together, that you cannot stick the point of the smallest needle into yourself any where, without hitting one of these little channels, and making the blood come.

This house wears out by using it all the time, and how is it to be repaired? You feel hungry, and this is the sign that it needs repairing. The earth and the waters give you food; the fire is ready to cook it. But some things are poison; but the nose is close by the mouth, and the eyes are there, and the taste is there, and all are ready to tell you whether you are about to eat poison. Who put these three witnesses just here, where they are most needed? Who made you feel *hungry*, so that the repairing the house should not be forgotten? Who put the *taste* in the mouth, so that you would *love* to eat? Who placed the teeth in the right place, to prepare the food for the stomach? You swallow your food, and there is a liquid in the stomach which will melt and eat it all away,—and which will eat any thing, except the stomach itself, and thus the food is made into blood, and then the heart drives it through the little channels into every part of the body. A part of it becomes bone, a part hair, a part flesh. What is not thus used goes into the lungs, where the air comes and washes it, and then away it goes again all over the body.

The body becomes weary, and is wearing down every day. But we have a physician to heal it. *Sleep* is that physician. It does not wait to be sent for; it comes whether we will or not. It does not come now and then, but statedly every day, because we every day need it. The heart beats, and the blood flows out every moment; but if *we* had to keep the heart beating, we could not sleep; or if we did, we should die during the first sleep.

If men had come into the world all clothed like a sheep, they could live only in the cold climates; if they had only a very thin covering, they could live only in the scorching climate where the camel lives; but they are born *naked*, so that they can clothe themselves for any climate. Was not this wise in God? Is not this house in which the soul lives a wonderful thing? How very wise must *He* be who made it!

Did you ever see an *elephant?* What a great head he carries—a head which weighs hundreds of pounds! So has the ox a great head; and these are to be held up, and off from the body, just as you would hold up a weight at arm's length. How do they support this heavy head? Why, there are two strong cords running along on the top of the neck, which fasten and hold the head to the back! *We* carry our head up straight, and do not need such cords; and we have none. Is not this wise?

The *oyster* cannot move to get out of the way, and why do not the fish eat him up? Because God has made his *bones* grow on the *outside!* The shell is the bone. The little *muscle* lives where the waters foam and dash, and how is he to be safe? He can spin little threads about half as long as my finger, and he often fastens himself to the rock by at least one hundred and fifty of these little cables! How wise was *He* who thus gave this frail little creature safe moorings amid the angry waters where it was born, and where is its home!

The little *bird* can dart through the woods, and hit twigs and limbs hundreds of times, and yet not hurt his eye. And the eagle can rise up and look the sun full in the face and not hurt his eye. How is this? Because they have a little covering for the eye, which they can draw down over it, and which is hard and able to keep it safe. This is a kind of *spectacle*, which shades and defends the eye, and yet allows the swift mover to see through it. Who made these curious spectacles?

The food must be ground before it can become blood. Most creatures have teeth to grind the food; but the little bird must have a small head, so that he can fly, and therefore he cannot have teeth; but God has given him a powerful little *mill* between the mouth and stomach, which can grind almost any thing, and prepare it for blood. It is called the *gizzard*; and wise was He who planned it.

The elephant goes naked. He can carry between three and four thousand pounds on his back. But if he had been placed at the north, he would have frozen to death. He has a curious trunk, as it is called, with which he can thread a needle, and do almost any thing which our hands can do. There are more than forty thousand little parts to this trunk, each one of which is under the direction of the elephant! What a wonderful machine!

The *reindeer* is covered with warm furs; this would kill him if he lived in a hot climate; but he lives in cold Greenland and Lapland, and his home and his dress are wisely made for each other.

The *whale* is born among the mountains of ice which hang around each pole. Why does he not freeze? Because God has wrapped him up in a great coat of fat, which in the thinnest places is at least two feet thick!

There is in the Indian seas, a fish of the oyster kind, called the *great clamp-fish*. One of them was caught which weighed five hundred and thirty-two pounds, and which fed one hundred and twenty men! Why do not the great fish eat up this delicious oyster? Because he can shut his shell together so tight as to cut the great cable of a ship in two. Who gave him this power by which to defend himself?

The pig, the cow, the horse, the sheep, and the goat, are the most useful creatures to men. They are wanted everywhere where men live. But all kinds of food will not grow everywhere. Now the fact is, there are seventy-two kinds of food which the pig will eat; two hundred and sixty-two which the horse will eat; two hundred and eighty-seven which the sheep will eat; and four hundred and forty-nine which the goat will eat. The consequence is, that, carry these creatures wherever they are wanted, and you will find some kind of food which they can eat.

What man could build a *ship* which could pass over the great sandy deserts of Africa? It could not sail like a ship on the water; it could not go on wheels like a stage. No man could build such a ship. But look at "the ship of the desert," which God has built. It can carry water in a bag, pure and sweet, which will last thirty days, and will go thirty miles a day for weeks together, and carry eight hundred pounds weight. It makes no noise. It never complains. Who made it? Ah! the *camel*, for this is "the ship of the desert," with his soft, spongy foot, just fitted for the sands of the desert, is made for this very business. The reindeer, in his soft furs, will bound over the snow and the ice a hundred miles a day; but if he and the camel were to exchange homes a single year, they would both die. The sands of the desert did not *make* the soft foot of the camel; nor did the foot make the sands; but God made them both, and fitted one for the other. Is not this wise?

The little bird which comes to your door sings sweetly, and his voice is always pleasant; but the bird which sits on the rock in the ocean, amid his stormy, lonely place, has no music in his voice. He has a shrill scream which can be heard above the roar of the storm, and through his noisy habitation.

You have heard of the *shark*. He is a hungry creature, and has been known to swallow iron, stones, wood, and even knives, and anything that you throw to him. Yet he is very nearsighted; and just before him swims a little fish, called the "pilot-fish," which sees the food and conducts the shark to it. But let the shark be ever so hungry, he will never hurt his little friend. Who taught him this? Again, the shark and the duck must both gather their food at the mouths of rivers, where the water is shoal; but let the shark be ever so hungry, he will not touch the duck, or any kind of fowl. Who planted this dislike to fowl in the shark? How wise is God in every thing!

A most curious workman can make a watch so small, that it can be placed in the ring which a lady wears upon her finger! How small and nice must each wheel and each part be! Now, there is not an insect which flies in the air, or creeps on the ground, which is not far more curious and wonderful in its make. A single insect has been found which had over four thousand parts, called muscles, each of which the little creature could call into use as he pleased! The world is full of such curious insects. They swim in our water,—they live in every thing. A learned French writer says, that he had a little strawberry-vine in a pot, in the window of his study, and in three weeks nearly forty different kinds of insects visited it, with which he became acquainted! These all have limbs, habits, characters, and homes of their own, as really as men have.

Did you ever hear of such a word as *instinct?* Do you know what an instinct is? The young hen has a brood of little chickens following her. She never saw a hawk in her life. She sees a small black speck in the sky, and at once utters the cry of danger. That little distant speck is a hawk. Her young chickens never heard her utter that cry before,—but they all run under her wings! Who taught them to do so? She utters another cry, and they come around her and pick up their food.

You have read of the *beaver*, have you not? When he wishes to make a pond, he goes to work to build a dam across the stream. He goes up the stream, and floats the timber down. Who told him that he could not float it *up*, as well as down? The stream is rapid and strong, and therefore he does not build his dam straight across the stream, but makes it *curve* up towards the stream! Who taught him that this curve would be stronger than a straight dam? God has so much wisdom, that he can lend of it to all the creatures which he has made.

Why does the little *bee* divide off her honeycomb into little regular cells? Who taught her that it would thus be stronger, than if all were made into one great basin? Who told her that if her honey were all put together into one place, it would turn sour and spoil? Does the bee reason all this out, or is it the wisdom of God which you see guiding her, so that she make no mistake?

All animals love their young, so long as they can teach them any thing; and this love ceases as soon as this is not the case, which is a very short time.

The infancy of man is long; and long does the mother watch and teach her child. Nor is this all. Let the child be a cripple, or sickly, or deformed, and does the mother turn away from it with loathing? Oh! no. She will watch and hang over it for years, and undergo danger or fatigue—which to others would be insupportable. And who planted such a love in the mother's bosom? And how wise was God, not only to plant such a love, but to order it so that the very trouble and anxiety should make it deeper and deeper!

Did you ever look off on the ocean? What a basin of waters! Ten thousand miles across one ocean! And all made salt, and rocked by the winds, and moved by the tides, lest they should become stagnant and spoiled! Do you know how the clouds are made, and where the rain and the hail comes from? I will tell you. The vapors rise up from the great ocean. The winds drive them to the land, and they become clouds. The cold makes it into hail or snow. It falls and waters the earth, and gives drink to men and to cattle, and then runs off in little brooks and great rivers into the ocean, again to rise and become clouds! How wonderful! So much *fresh* water to be continually made from water that is salt!

This is the birthplace of rains and dews, which bless the earth so much. Without the ocean, we should all perish at once, and there would be neither grass nor flower, man, nor beast, nor bird, on the whole earth! And as to food, it is supposed that more people live by what comes out of the sea, than there are who live by what comes from the land itself.

Suppose in making men God had made every face alike! What child could know his parents? Who would know their neighbors? Who would know an honest man from a thief or a robber? How could it be known, when a man was robbed or murdered, who did it? Was it not wise so to make men, that no two look alike?

No two men are made so exactly alike, that they can *write* exactly alike. If you had a paper here, containing the handwriting of every man living, you would see that no two write exactly alike. This prevents our having counterfeits and forgeries; for if every man could write just as all the rest do, there could be no such thing as doing business.

The tongue tells others what we think; and the ear tells us what others say to us; and were it not for these two little members, we should be but little, if any, better than apes.

Was it not wise in God to give us the sun to pour down his light and heat,—to measure off the seasons, and to give us summer and winter?

But we cannot study all the time, nor work all the time; and so God has provided day and night, that we might have labour and rest just as often as we need it, all our life long. Is not this wise?

But what wisdom does God show in the *Bible*!

He wanted to tell us who and what he is; and so he taught good men all what he is, and what we are. He told these good men to write it all, so that it might be kept from age to age: and lest we should say, We don't know that he sent them, and told them to write the book, he gave them power to prove that he *did* send them, by working miracles,—such wonders as making the sun and the moon stand still; opening the sea for his people to walk through it; healing the sick, awaking the dead, and the like.

He knew that we were all sinners, and that we could never of ourselves become holy, and come back to him; and so he sent his only Son, Jesus Christ, to come down to this world, to teach it, to die to save it, and then to rise from the dead and go up to heaven, and there take care of his people. I could tell you much about this Saviour. The Bible is full of him; and I hope the time may come, when I shall be able to speak to you about him again. I mention it now, because God will show his wisdom to all heaven, more by his redeemed church which will be gathered from the earth, than in any other way, and in all other ways.

Wicked men, and prayerless men, see no wisdom in sending Jesus Christ to save this world. Praying men see a great deal. They think about this more than about all other things. They have stronger and sweeter hopes connected with this, than with any other subject. When they go to the house of God on the Sabbath, it is to learn about this Saviour: when they die, like Stephen when he was stoned to death, Acts 7:60, they commit their souls to him. And in heaven, where all the angels are, and where prophets, and apostles, and all good men who have gone up from this world are, they will see Jesus, and praise him, and there admire the wisdom of God more and more for ever.

But this is not all I would say. These beautiful heavens are all to be destroyed. The sun is to be put out. So is the moon. The stars are all to fade away in darkness. This charming world is all to be burned up and turned into ashes. All to be thrown away. But God will then build new heavens and a new earth,—more perfect, more beautiful than this. It will be made to stand for ever. What wisdom will there be seen! *Here*, the body has pains and aches: *there*, it will never have pain. Here, we must be fed every day, or we starve: there, we can live and neither hunger nor thirst. Here, we grow old, and decay, and die: there, we shall never grow old, never become feeble, never die. Here, we have fears and anxieties, disappointments and griefs: there, we shall be free from all these, for the former things have passed away.

Oh! if here, in a world where sin is, and sorrow is, and where every thing tells us that our life is but for a moment, there are so many marks of the wonderful wisdom of God, how will it be in that world where the fullness of his wisdom will be seen!

The father takes out his knife and cuts his little boy a stick, or makes him a top—because he is a child; but is this stick or this top any thing to what he will do for that child when he becomes a man, and needs a house? No. But when he comes to build the house for his son, you will see how he will plan it, and build it, and make it very perfect and very complete. So with God. What he gives us here are only a few playthings, as it were; but when we come to go to him, in his eternal kingdom, what will he not give us? Oh! if you love and obey his Son, what wisdom will you not then see? "Eye hath not seen, ear hath not heard, neither hath it entered into the heart of man, the things which he hath prepared for those who love him." May you all be there, and see and enjoy it all. Amen.

LECTURE 6.—GOD KNOWS EVERYTHING

WHO INSTRUCTED HIM?—Isa 40:14

St. Paul's Cathedral—Christopher Wren—Shipbuilding—The telescope—Wooden man—How *we* know—How *God* knows—The bird—The oak—The eye—First proof—*God knows what men will do*—Saul the king—Cyrus—No low notions of God—Mahomet—The nations—Second proof—*God knows what men will think*—Third proof—*God will judge the world*—The Jews—The murdered man—No concealment—What we call knowledge—Real knowledge—How men think—Instruction 1.—*God not disappointed*—The tower—Great plans—Wicked plans—Who disappointed—Instruction 2.—*God does no injustice*—How we do men injustice—Innocent man hanged—We do God injustice—Instruction 3.—*The good rewarded*—Joseph—Job—Martyrs—The father—Mother—Daughter—The bright boy—Instruction 4.—*We ought to be afraid to sin*—Day of judgment—what?—Things brought out—God looks deep in the heart—Conclusion.

Did any of these many children present ever hear of a building called *St. Paul's Cathedral?* It is in London, and it is very large, very high, and very beautiful. When people wish to have a view of the whole city, they go up to the top and look down. It is so high, that men look like little insects, as they walk along the streets, and the carriages seem no larger than those in the toyshops.

Did you ever hear who planned and built that wonderful building? His name was Christopher Wren; and his name will be known to children who shall live thousands of years after you and I are dead. How could he rear such a building? Because he had seen a thousand buildings before this, and he had studied the buildings and the plans which other minds in other ages had formed.

When a man would build a great ship, he cannot sit down and form the plan of a ship, and then go and put it together. No. He must go to somebody who has seen many ships, and planned many, and who has made it his study for years. And then we think him to be a great man who can build a ship.

You have heard of a long tube through which men look when they want to see the stars plainly,—have you not? Can any one of these little boys tell me the name of it? Who can? *"Telescope"*—that little girl with a brown bonnet on her head says.—Very well. When a man first made a telescope, it was considered a wonderful thing: but the man *copied* something. Do you know what it was? It was the *eye* of a man! and the telescope is perfect and right, if it comes near being like the eye.

They have, too, a kind of wooden man, which they carry round to show. He can play on the flute, or violin,—because he is filled with little wires and springs, which move his fingers and make him play. But those who make these things only *copy*. They see men, and copy as well as they can; but after all, they can't make one that can walk, and talk, and read, and *think*, as you can.

I am going to show you that God knows every thing—every thing that ever *has* been, that now is, that *will* be, or that *can* be.

When we know any thing, it is because we have seen it, or heard it, have examined and studied it, and taken pains to learn about it. But when, God knows things, he does not have to glance the eye,—before we could glance the eye, he sees and knows every thing.

When God created things, he had no plan,—no model,—no one to tell him how to contrive, or how to make them.

Who told him that fire would give out heat and light—before fire was made? Who told him that water would put out fire, and be good for men and cattle to drink when they feel thirsty, and good to make the grass and trees green? Who told him that the air would be good to breathe, good to make every thing live, even to the little blue violet that peeps its head up in the crack of the rock?

How did God know how to make the little bird so that she could balance herself on her wings away up in the air, rising up to the very clouds? Who told him that her wing must be made of feathers, and not of lead, and that the wing must have a joint in it, and not be one straight bone?

Who drew the size and the shape of the great oak, or of the apple-tree, before a tree was ever seen? Who "taught him" how to make a house for the soul to live in, its shape, and size, and limbs, as your body is made? Who told him that a spirit could be put into such a house made of the dust of the ground, and live there?

Your eye lets light, and the picture of houses and trees, and every beautiful thing you see, into the soul; but no eye had ever been seen when God created it! Your ear has curious little chambers, so that you can hear sweet sounds and sweet music; but no ear had ever been seen when God made the ear of Adam! Ah! if God could thus make the heavens, and the earth, and the great sea, and all things, feed all, and clothe all, and take care of all, and do all this before day, or night, or sun, or moon, or light was made, must it not be *that he knows everything?*

God knows what men will do before they know themselves.

He sent Moses to the great and wicked king of Egypt, and told him to let his people go;—and he knew exactly what the king would do. He knew he would be wicked, and say No. He knew just when he would yield, after the ten plagues had been sent;—that he would follow Israel into the Red Sea, and there be drowned. Read this wonderful account in Exodus 1-14.

Saul was the first king of Israel, and God knew before he was made king just what he would do, and how he would behave. He knew that Solomon would be a great and a wise king, and would build the great and beautiful temple at Jerusalem.

Hundreds of years before Cyrus was born, God knew that he would be born, that he would have that name, and do just as Cyrus did.

You all know how Judas sold Jesus Christ for a little money; how Pilate and Herod killed him; but for hundreds of years before they did these things God knew it all, and told men that they would do it,—told for how many pieces of money Christ should be sold,—how he should die,—how be buried,—how long lie in the tomb, and that he would rise again. All this God knew from eternity. But we must not have low thoughts of God, and suppose that he *determined* all this should be done, and then *made* men do it whether they would or not! Oh, no! God never *makes* men sin; but he knew that they would choose to do it.

How could God know that Mahomet, that false Arabian prophet, should be born, and should deceive so many people? Did you ever read the Book of Daniel? There are some most beautiful stories in it, and some things hard to be understood; but this we can see, that in that book God has foretold that many different nations and kingdoms would rise up, hundreds of years before they were ever known. Again, he knew and told when and how they should again perish and be no more. There he tells about the ruin of great Babylon and Persia,—about Alexander, the great murderer,—about Rome, which was like an image whose foot was made of iron and clay,—and about the coming of his dear Son, Jesus Christ. How could God tell all these things so long before they took place, except that he knows every thing?

God knows what men think, and what they will think, before they know themselves.

He made the heart, and put it all in motion, and does he not know what is going on in the heart? How could he know that wicked Judas would sell his Master for just thirty pieces of money, unless he knew just how much he would love money, and just what he would think about it? "There is not a word upon the tongue, nor a thought in the heart, but, lo! it is altogether known unto thee."

How did he know that there would be men who would scoff, and say, "Where is the promise of his coming?"—unless he knew just what these men would think? And

The fact that God will judge all men, shows that he knows everything.

Men have been in this world nearly six thousand years, and all this time there have been millions living and dying. When the end will come, we do not know, nor does an angel in heaven. But the end *will* come, and then *all* are to be judged. And who are *all?*

The wicked spirits who were cast out of heaven are to be judged;—the men who lived before the flood, those giants in sin, are all to be judged;—every deed that each one of all these has done is to be called up and judged.

The Jews who lived and sinned with the Bible in their hands, and the Gentiles who never had the Bible, but whose conscience told them they were doing wrong—all must be judged.

The last year, a man was murdered over in the western part of Philadelphia, near the Schuylkill, and it took all the constables, and officers, and judges many weeks to find out all about it, and get the testimony, and to *judge* who did it, and what punishment he ought to receive. What labour! What expense to find out and punish *one* single sin!

But God will bring to light all that is now forgotten, and covered up. Not a man ever lived on earth, but all he was, all he did, all he thought, and wished, and felt, will be known to God, and by him told to the world. Men may sin in secret, in the darkness of night,—they may conceal their sins, deny them,—but God will make every sin stand out in open light, as plainly as if painted on canvass. What knowledge must he have! Verily, "hell is naked before him, and destruction hath no covering." [Job 26:6]

When we think or speak of a man of *knowledge*, we think of a being who has lived but a few days,—who has read a little in books,—has studied a little, thought a little, and who knows a very little more than to feed his own body! This we call knowledge! Alas! it is only the small light of a little taper.

But *He*, who before any single thing was made, saw and knew the pattern and likeness of every thing,—every star, and sun, and man, and bird, and beast, and fish, and insect,—who knows every little string in the body, and every power of the mind,—who knows what will be the condition, the feelings, the wishes, the thoughts, of every man who will ever live,—who holds in the grasp of his mighty hand all things, all changes, great and small, dark and light, good and bad,—who can see all, know all, weigh all, *judge* all, and make all turn to his glory,—he has knowledge! This is not the light of the taper: it is the sun.

Some men think that if they can only get away out of the sight of men, they may sin as much as they please. In this way, some go to work and make counterfeit money; some deceive in their bargains;—some have feelings and wicked wishes in their hearts, and think it is no matter if no man knows it. But such men must not think that they can do any thing, or go any where, or wish any thing, and have it concealed from God. No. He knows every thing, and you might as well try to live without breathing, as to try to do, or think, or feel wrong, and not have God know it. He can neither be taught nor deceived.

I might go on with more proof that God knows every thing, but I trust I have made it plain to you; and now I am wishing that these children should learn some things which we *may* learn from this subject. And you learn,

1. *That God can never be disappointed.*

Oh! how many created beings have been disappointed! Those bright angels who once stood near the throne of God in heaven, thought they might sin, and yet still do well. How little did they think their sins would cast them into hell for ever! And yet they have been disappointed. They may be very many, and very cunning, and very powerful, and very resolute, but God knows all their plans, and can turn them all against themselves; and by a hand too mighty for them to resist, he can crush all their hopes!

Some men once thought they would build a tower, and make to themselves a great name; but the Lord comes down and disappoints them, and their Babel cannot go up high towards heaven, as they hoped it would.

Men sometimes lay great plans, and have much gold, and many great minds, and great armies to help them carry out their plans, and the Lord blows upon them, just as you would blow out a lamp, and they are all disappointed! But it is not so with God.

Judas may go mad, and go out into the lonely field and hang himself; Pilate and Herod may become friends in order to kill the Saviour; and it is not new to God. He knew it all before these men were born. Infidels sometimes take their pen and write a book, sometimes a large book, and sometimes a small one, by which they try to make men believe that the Bible did not come from God;—and the smallest child here might as well try to blow down the great mountain with his breath. No, no! Others may be disappointed, may sit down and wring their hands in anguish, may have their hearts ache over their sorrows; but the plans, the designs of God, will all come out just as he wishes, and he will never be disappointed in regard to anything.

2. *You learn that God will never do any body any injustice.*

We are in danger of doing injustice to our fellow men. We do not know just what is their situation, and thus we say that such a man ought to do so and so, or he ought to alter his course. But perhaps if we were in *their* situation, we should do just as they do.

A dishonest man is apt to think that all men are dishonest. Thus he does them injustice. A sour, ill-natured man, thinks that all feel just as he does. The man who envies others, thinks that all do so too. These all do men injustice. Sometimes, too, we blame men unjustly, when they do as well as they can, though we may not, and do not, know it; and it is almost impossible that we should think and feel towards any man as we should, if we knew just what was in his heart.

A few years ago a man was tried for murder in England, and was hung for it, when it afterwards was found out that no murder had ever been committed in that town. And a man in Vermont came very near being put to death for murdering a man, when the man was alive, and was found alive, and brought in and shown to the court. But this can never be in God's dealings with men.

We may do *him* injustice,—we may say he is not a wise God,—or that he is not so good as we should like,—or we may doubt his truth,—

we may break his laws,—blaspheme his name,—despise, his holiness,—
scorn his word,—we may do any or all of this injustice towards him, for
we are ignorant and sinful beings;—but *he* can never do injustice. He
sees the angel when he covers his face with his wings in heaven; he
knows his heart, and the heart of every angel, of every man, and of every
child that ever lived, or ever will live; and he cannot,—will not, do
injustice to any one, in this life, or in the next.

3. *You learn that God will reward all who do well, because he knows all that
they do.*

Joseph had rather go to prison than to sin; and he did go, and was
shut up for years, rather than sin;—but it was because he felt that God
knew all about him, and would reward him.

Job was covered with disease,—his property all swept away,—and
his children all buried under the house which the wind had blown down
upon them; his wife tried to make him sin, and his best friends gave him
bitter words—and yet he sinned not, because he knew that God knew
all about it, and would reward him.

You have heard of martyrs, have you not? Some of them were sawn
in two by a great saw; some were driven away into the cold mountains,—
some were shot, some stabbed, and some torn in pieces by wild beasts,
which had been shut up and almost starved, on purpose to make them
fierce and cruel. If you had been in Rome at one time, you might have
seen many thousands covered with pitch and tar, and burned to death,
and sometimes they were burned in the night, to be seen better.

There, the father was shut in prison, away from his family,
tomorrow to be burned, because he will not worship an idol, and deny
the Saviour.

There, the mother knelt on the cold stones in the dungeon, and
prayed for her babes, whom she was to leave alone, for tomorrow she
must die by being burned at the stake.

There, the daughter was led out, and the lions tore her in pieces,
because she would not sin against God; and there the bright Christian
boy, no older than many of you, was led between the soldiers, as he
went to be crushed and torn by the wild beasts;—and yet his little step
was light and firm, and his sweet eye was bright, and his young face was
cheerful—because he believed that God knew every thing, and would
reward him. Ah! and so he will. He knows all our sorrows and trials, our
tears and sighs over our sins, and he will remember his promises, and
will hereafter, in his kingdom, reward us abundantly.

4. If God knows everything, then we see what a great day the judgment-day will be.

There will be a most wonderful sight at the great day of judgment. We know but little of what men do and say and feel that is wrong, but God knows all.

Much of the wickedness of men has been covered up by the ages that have gone past; character is concealed by partial friends; it is covered up by shame; it is bought into good repute by gold; it is winked at by us as an excuse for our sins:—but in the day when God comes to judge the world, and to bring out every character as it stands in *his* sight, it will not be so. What has been buried by years, or concealed by the grave, will come out, and all stand out as fresh as if it were done but yesterday. God knows it all, and will bring it all out, and show it all, and then punish it all. That which friends covered, will be covered no longer. That which shame put away in the corner, will be put away no longer. Wrongs which we have not dreamed of will come to light. Oh! what a scene will that day be! Ah! and those sins which you commit in your childhood, and those habits which you now begin to fix upon yourselves like chains, and which will shortly become your masters,—these will all be brought into judgment by the knowledge of God.

That young heart that now knows how to sin, to deceive, to have burning passions within it,—must be laid open.

Ah! if God would only look at your outside,—if he would recall only such sins as you remember,—if he would only deal with you for those sins which the eye of man only has seen!—but alas! this is not it! God knows every thing; and he will bring you into judgment for all that you have been, now are, or ever will be,—your words, thoughts, and the feelings of your heart! Say, are you not afraid to sin?

When these dear children have slept the sleep of ages,—when they have been called up from the grave by the angel of the resurrection, to be judged for all that they are, or do, or ever will do,—for sins committed in secret, and sins open and known, what will they do? The rocks cannot cover you, the hills cannot fall on you,—for the rocks and the hills are melted, the sea is dried up and is no more, every island has fled away, and there is nothing left but the blessed Redeemer; but you must *now* make him your friend,—you must *now* obey him, serve him, love him, or he will not then save you. Amen.

LECTURE 7.—GOD'S POWER

AH LORD GOD! BEHOLD, THOU HAST MADE THE
HEAVENS AND THE EARTH BY THY GREAT POWER AND
STRETCHED-OUT ARM, AND THERE IS NOTHING TOO
HARD FOR THEE.—Jer 32:17

Village of Anathoth—Jeremiah in prison—Curious time to buy a farm—
Power of God—How first seen—A grain of wheat—The great ball—Great
basin—Great channel dug—The mountains—Small creatures—The balloon—
Going to the sun in a balloon—Going to the stars—Candle in a star—Number of
stars—How God makes things—*Mind's* great chain—Changes of this world—
Second way of seeing God's power—Kings—*Mind is power*—Three things showing
the power of God—*The first thing*—The happy family—Sorrows come—The
widow's God—*Second thing showing God's power*—Wonderful examples—God
governs the minds of men—Greatness of Babylon—*Third thing showing God's
power*—Satan and Christ—Christ in the manger—Christ on the cross—Christ in the
tomb—God's strength—The flood—Nebuchadnezzar—What is an inference?—
First inference—We can give the Bible to the world—Difficulties in the way—*Second
inference*—Faith in God—Wicked are under God—*Third inference*—God terrible to the
wicked—How he can punish—*Last inference*—*God's power should make the good
happy*—What protection!—Conclusion.

There was a little village a few miles from Jerusalem, and its name
was Anathoth. Jeremiah was born there, and there his relations lived.

By the laws of Moses, when a man wished to sell his farm, he must
first offer it to his nearest relations, to see if they wished to buy it.

At the time the words of my text were written, the great army of the
Chaldeans was in Anathoth. Jeremiah had come to Jerusalem, to tell the

king and all the people, that for their sins God was going to give them into the hands of the Chaldeans for seventy long years. They were so much displeased with Jeremiah, that they shut him up in a prison, and put his feet in the stocks. In a short time he knew that Jerusalem would be taken, and all burned up, and all the people carried away captives to Babylon. While these things were so, a relation came to Jeremiah, to ask him to buy his small farm that was in Anathoth! What a time to buy an estate!

But God tells Jeremiah to make the purchase, and have it recorded. The prophet does so. If his heart fails him, he comforts himself with the words of my text: "Ah Lord God! behold, thou hast made the heaven and the earth by thy great power and stretched-out arm, and there is nothing too hard for thee."

Children, I am now going to speak to you about the *power of God*, and I want you to sit very still, and to be careful to hear all I have to say. Though I can, at this time, mention only a few things which show the power of God, yet the things which do show it, are all around us everywhere.

1. *Look at the power of God in what he has made.*

A little child can take a grain of wheat and drop it into the earth,— by the aid of the earth, the air, the sun, the rain, and the dew, it grows and fills the ear of wheat. By a little grinding at the mill, the coarse and fine parts are separated, and you have flour. By a little adding of water, and by baking, you have bread. You eat the bread, and it becomes flesh, and blood, and bone.

But suppose *you* had to do all this! Could you make the grain of wheat? Could you make it grow when made? Could you make it turn into blood, and bone, and flesh? What power of God is seen in every grain of wheat!

Suppose there never had been a grain of sand, nor a single atom of dust, could *you* make the smallest dust that ever floated in the sunbeam? Could all the men in the world do it? No. But God could make this world, a great ball, so large, that if a hole were dug through it, and an apple were dropped into the hole, it must fall *eight thousand miles* before it gets through!

You can bring two drops of water together, and you might; by great digging and much hard work, turn the channel of the small brook, and make the brook run in a different place; but could you make a basin of waters *ten thousand miles* across its top, and so deep that no man can measure it, even with the longest rope? Could you make such basins again and again, till all the oceans on the earth were made? Could you dig great channels, some of them many miles wide, and fill them all with waters, and thus make all those great rivers which pour their waters on towards the great ocean, and which will thus run as long as the world lasts? No, you cannot; no man can; but God can do all this!

If somebody would bring you the things, perhaps you might build a pile as large as a load of hay; but how would you go to work to rear up a mountain, and many mountains, some of which are five miles high, and hundreds of miles long? their tops covered with snow that never melts, and great fires under them which make them shake like a sick man? Oh! what power must God have, to do all this!

Men can shoot a bird on the wing; they can subdue the horse and the elephant; they can spear the fish, and crush the insect with the foot. But who has power to *make* the smallest insect that creeps or flies, or the most tiny fish that swims? God can do all this. The little creeper, too small for your eye to see, as he sits on the leaf, and is rocked by the winds, cries to God, and is heard by God as plainly as the angel in heaven before his throne! He gives life, and breath, and food, to all that walk or creep, or fly or swim, though all the men in the world could not keep one of them alive for a single day.

You have heard of a balloon. It is a great bag made of silk, and filled with light air. It can rise up in the air towards the clouds with a man in it. I have seen one with a man in it, which was at least a mile high.

Now, suppose you could ride in a balloon day and night, and go as fast as a ball shot from a cannon, how long do you think it would take you to reach the sun? *Twenty-five years!* How large would you find it? Why, it would take a *million and a half* of such worlds as this, to make one world as large as the sun! And yet God moves or stops the sun just as he pleases! Suppose, now, you could leave the sun in your balloon, and sail off to the nearest star, how long would it take to get there, going as fast as a cannonball? It would take you *six hundred thousand years!*

Suppose when you had got to the nearest star, you should light a candle which *we* could see here in this world; how long would it be after the candle was lighted, before it could be seen in this world? *Three years and seventy-nine days!*

And how many such stars are there? Ah! we do not know; we only know that there are more than *one hundred millions,* and probably these are only a small part of what God has made! Yet "*He* telleth the number of the stars, and he calleth them by name." No wonder he says in the Bible, "Lift up your eyes on high, and behold!"

But *how* does God make and uphold all these great worlds? "He speaks, and it is done"—a world is created. He calls for light, and it breaks out of what was eternal darkness, and hangs around the world as a mother hangs over her babe. He speaks again, and the waters roll off, and the dry land rises up. He reaches forth his hand, and hangs the sun, the moon, and the stars up in their places. "He made the stars also"— not as *we* make things: no: "he spake, and it was done; he commanded, and it stood fast."

Yet there is something more bright and glorious than the brightest sun and the purest star: it is the *minds* which God has made; *minds*, which fill earth with cities, and the seas with ships, and which will live, and think, and feel, and act, for ever and ever!

Suppose you could see a chain held in the hand of God, which holds every weed and flower, every insect and creature, that lives, every mind that thinks, whether in this or in any other world, would you not feel that the hand of God was strong, to hold all up, every moment, from the morning of creation, to the end of all things? "He fainteth not, neither is he weary." "There is nothing too hard for the Lord." Men are born and die; trees grow up and fall away; nations grow and perish; but all the works of God continue as they were from the beginning, because from age to age God remains the same, almighty in power, unaltered, undiminished, untired, unceasing! What a being God is!

2. *Look at the power of God as he governs the world.*

God made the body, and the spirit in the body, and knows just how to reach and guide the spirit. Herod and Pilate may lay their plans just as will please themselves; and the wicked in hell may curse and swear day and night for ever, if they wish; but God knows how to make all this wickedness turn, so as to bring honour to his own name.

You know, children, that your father sometimes tells you to do things which you do not wish to do; yet you do them, and obey his will. But God can make people obey his will, and *wish* to do it at the same time. Even the greatest kings that lift up themselves against him, are only the saw lifting up itself against him that shaketh with it, and the axe that riseth up against him that heweth with it.

When you lift your hand to your head, it is your will that moves it. When you raise your foot, it is because your *will* moves it: and when you move any part of your body, is it not your *will* that does it? Just so God moves every part of creation. *Mind is power*. The strongest man that ever lived could not raise a finger, if his mind be gone. He is then dead. The moon or the great sun could not move an inch, unless God moves them.

Now see, children, if when you get home you remember and tell your friends *three things* which show God's power in governing his creatures.

1. *He can make great joy to come from great sorrows*.

Suppose you know a family who live in a great, beautiful house, surrounded by trees, with a large garden, and everything pleasant. They have a fine family of children. The father and mother are both pious people, and are doing all they can to train up their children for the service of God. They are the happiest family you know of.

But times change. By great losses of money, they become poor. They must leave their beautiful house, and costly furniture, and go and live in a small, poor house. Then the father is taken sick, and after months of great pain and suffering he dies, and is buried in the grave, and is gone for ever. The mother is now left poor, with nothing but her orphan children and her God. To whom can she now look? Where will she now find a covering from the storm?

She goes to God,—she clings to his word: she trusts to him who is the widow's God, and a father to the fatherless. She now finds that she has been too long drinking of the waters of earth, and forgetting the waters of life. She leans upon God, is guided by him, and has new peace and joy poured into her bosom. In her little cottage, with her children, she calls upon God. They sing his praises, and God gives to this family such peace as they knew not before. He can bring joy out of sorrow, and make the thorn which goes deep into the flesh cause great happiness. The beautiful story of Joseph in Genesis, will show you what I mean. Will you read it?

2. *The power of God can keep his people when in dangers*.

A wicked king with a great army of soldiers once followed God's people, and he opened the Red Sea, and made the waters stand up on each side like a wall.

Twice he made the waters gush out of the hard rock in the wilderness, that his people might have drink.

They would have starved during the forty years in the wilderness, had not God, every morning, created manna enough for three millions of people to eat.

When the people of God got into the land of Canaan, they had heathen nations all around them, who wanted to make war upon them and destroy them; and the Jews had the command of God that all the *men* should go up to Jerusalem three times every year to worship him. Now why did not these heathen come down upon them in armies and destroy them, while the men were all gone away to Jerusalem? Because God so governed their *minds*, that they had no *wish* to do it. He can chain up the *wishes* of men. You know how he did it when the prison doors were thrown open, and the prisoners did not wish to escape, Acts 16.

Once the people of God were slaves in Babylon. The greatest king on earth was their master. The walls of Babylon were *fifty feet* thick, and *one hundred and fifty feet* high, and the gates were of solid brass. How could they get out? God can open a way. He creates Cyrus, the Persian, who comes with a great army, opens the gates, reads in the Bible what the prophets said about him more than one hundred years before this, and he worships God, and at once sends the captive people back to Jerusalem.

Wicked men have many times tried to destroy the people of God. Even kings and rulers have tried to do it; but what did they do? "He that sitteth in the heavens shall laugh,—the Lord shall hold them in derision."

3. *The power of God is seen in turning the plans of Satan, the greatest sinner, against himself.*

Hundreds of years before Jesus Christ came to this world, it was told that he would come. He was to be the heir of the world. And how did the wicked one rejoice, when he saw him a poor man, despised by men, with no friends but a few poor fishermen! Is *this* "the desire of the nations?" Ah! how did he rejoice! And how was he amazed, when he saw that these poor fishermen could preach with a power which nobody could answer! and with a boldness which prisons and death could not check!

How did Satan rejoice when he saw the Son of God, the heir of the world, cradled in a manger, and King Herod ordering all the babes in Bethlehem to be murdered! And how was he baffled, when he saw the wise men of the East come to worship him, and a new star created to do him honor!

Christ was taken by wicked men and nailed to the cross, and shut up in the tomb, all sealed up: and doubtless there was joy in the dark world of sin; but oh! the power of the cross! It spoiled these principalities and powers; it is rivers of waters to the perishing soul on the sands of India; it is the "Wonderful, Counselor, mighty God, everlasting Father, Prince of Peace," to the Indian in the wilderness,—it is the morning star to the wanderer in darkness and in sin,—it is the power of God to all who believe!

The soldiers were there, and the seal was on the tomb, and the great stone was on the mouth; but Christ arose from the dead. Satan now persuaded the Jews to reject him, and not to believe him,—and he thought he had done a great and a wicked work. They tried to kill the Christians, and have Christ forgotten! But oh! what power has God! The Christians were driven away from their homes, and they went every where preaching the word! and thus thousands and millions of poor Gentiles have been led to look unto "the Lamb of God which taketh away the sins of the world."

The weakness of God is stronger than the strength of men. Suppose you see a man frown. What does that frown do? It only shows that he is displeased. But when God frowns, the heavens tremble, "yea, they perish at the rebuke of his countenance."

Suppose a man lift his finger,—what can he do with a finger? But with the finger of God devils are controlled, and by his fingers the heavens were made.

What power must he have, to roll the flood over every valley, and hill, and mountain! What power, to rain fire and brimstone upon the five cities, and thus make their smoke go up, as the smoke of a great furnace!

Ah! God can hurl the army of Egypt into the Red Sea, and drown them all. He can turn the heart of Nebuchadnezzar into the heart of a beast, and make the proudest man to become a beast!

There is nothing too hard for the Lord. His hand will open every grave, and bring up every sleeper. His breath shall kindle a fire which shall burn up this world, and these heavens; and then, from their ashes will he build up new heavens and a new earth, which shall stand for ever!

Children, do you know what an *inference* is? I will tell you. If you can *prove* to me that the little boy there, who is so attentive, is a kind and obedient child, then, I *infer*, that his parents love him very much. This is an *inference*.

So now, having *proved* that God has almighty power, I *infer* some things.

1. *I infer that he can aid us to carry the Bible to all people.*

Give the Bible to all people! Unbelief cries, "If the Lord would make windows in heaven, then might this thing be!" "How can he give us his flesh to eat?"

The power of God answers, "Fear not, little flock, it is your Father's good pleasure to give you the kingdom." Aided by this power, the stripling Joseph becomes the savior of Egypt; Moses, the son of a poor slave, becomes the leader of Israel; David, the shepherd's boy, becomes the king of Israel, and "the sweet singer" of the church of God. The mustard-seed becomes a great tree.

The religion of the heathen is as old as the flood; the religion of the Mohammedans is fierce, cruel, and bloody; the religion of the Jews is cold, selfish, blind, and stubborn; but the power of God will raise up many souls, to live, and preach, and pray, and weep, and by them the world will be brought back to God. We may seem small, and feeble, and poor; but Christ sits in the heavens, and has all power in heaven and on earth, and he will help his people to carry the gospel to every creature under heaven.

I infer,

2. *That the power of God gives us faith in his government.*

There are good men who look to God to guide them through life; to go with them, and lead them safely through the regions of death;—to raise them up from the grave, and make them blessed for ever: and God will do it all, for nothing is too hard for him.

There are wicked men who do not love God; who hate his Bible; they do not pray to God; they try to destroy his Sabbath, and make the world hate his church. But God can say even to the roaring waves, "Hitherto shalt thou come, and no further." He can melt away a nation, and crush it by war, by hunger, or even by a locust or a worm. Who can thunder like him? He fears no man;—he is almighty in power, and can do as he pleases. Such wicked men as Pharaoh, Herod, and Pilate, he laughs into silence for ever.

I infer,

3. *That the power of God is terrible to wicked people.*

What an eye God has! No darkness can hide from it; no cave shut it out! Go to heaven, and he is there! Go to hell, and he is there! Fly away on the wings of morning light, and he gets there before you! Nay, he himself must help you to fly. "I will render vengeance to mine enemies, and reward them that hate me!" Ah! what can he not do to the wicked! He can throw a little speck of dust in your eye, and you are in great pain. His finger can touch a single cord in the brain, and you rave with madness. He can fill the soul full of terrors, and fears, and horror. What then will bad men do, when God makes a business of punishing? If Judas was so wretched here, that he chose to murder himself, how will he feel when God comes to teach him that it had been "better for him had he never been born?" When the great God comes to deal with wicked men, how will they feel? Through what door will they run? What arm can deliver them? Oh! how will he tread them down in his fury, and put them to shame and everlasting contempt!

Dear children, every time we sin, we say unto God, that we dare his power; but, oh! when he judges us, we shall be like briers and thorns before the great fire! "Do we provoke the Lord to anger? Are we stronger than he?"

I infer,

4. *That the power of God should make his people feel happy.*

Suppose one of these children be a holy child, and a friend of Christ,—still, what dangers are around him! He is but a poor little child, only a few years old, like a worm crushed before the moth; the worm is his sister and mother, and the grave will soon be his home. He has a wicked heart, too, within him. Can he ever get through this world of sin, through the grave, and reach heaven? Yes. I hear a voice saying, "All things are yours." "I am persuaded that neither death, nor life, nor angels, nor principalities, nor powers, nor things present, nor things to come, nor height, nor depth, nor any other creature, shall be able to separate us from the love of God in Christ Jesus our Lord."

Children, that house in which your soul now lives, (I mean your body,) must be taken down and put into the grave; but don't be afraid; the power of God will raise it up again, glorious, beautiful, undying. The grave must be your sleeping-place; but do not fear it; the power of God shall open it and bring up your dust into life. This world must be burned up; but do not fear; the power of God will rear up another, more beautiful and more perfect than this. That bright sun must go out; but do not fear; God will make eternity take the place of time, and his own face shall be our sun for ever! All will go and perish; but you, little ones, you may take hold of the arm of God, and that arm will lift you over every snare, and lead you up to a world which is full of joy. Amen.

LECTURE 8.—TRUTH OF GOD

———————

Honest men and knaves not alike—Truth very important—What if God be not true?—A wish for these children—God a being of truth—*First proof*—A deceitful father—How we are made—The argument—Continued—God a being of truth—*Second proof*—May men ever deceive?—Boy about to be killed—Why may he not deceive?—False balance—God a being of truth—*Third proof*—The Flood—Rainbow—Summer and winter—The Dead Sea—Passover—Sin and misery connected—No dishonest man happy—Story of a dishonest man—Every sin makes us unhappy—God a being of truth—*Fourth proof*—Abraham—David—Captivity—God a being of truth—*Fifth proof*—Gehazi—Story of the three robbers—Lying despised—Lying brings certain ruin—How God views lying—God a being of truth—*Last proof*—When men deceive—How men are tempted—Change views—Men have prejudices—Men deceive because poor—God above all want—God sincere—One single *inference*—The angel—One great pillar—Men in trouble—Paul—Stephen the martyr—The little child—The storm—The grave—Feeling sins—Short prayer.

Some men are honest, and just, and sincere; some are knaves, and cheats, and liars. Would you suppose that God, who loves justice and truth, would let these men be equal in this world? He does not.

The honest man speaks the *truth* at all times, and this is the wisest way, even for this life. The knave doesn't see this, and so he tells *lies*. This point of true wisdom is hid from the bad man, and so he is not equal to the good man. God has hid it from his eyes.

If truth be so important between men, how vastly important is it between God and men? For all our hopes, which reach beyond the grave, rest upon *the truth of God,*—and this we call an everlasting foundation.

Suppose it were so, that God is not a being of truth, then must every hope perish like a withered rose. This life may not be real,—only a dream, and all beyond the grave looks dark and fearful, and full of despair. If he be not a being of perfect truth, then all we have read about him in the Bible is false,—all we have read about Christ is false,—and all we have read about sin, and repentance, and salvation, is false. There is no heaven for the good, no hell for the wicked, no judgment to try men.

Who would try to live for heaven, if there be no such thing; and who would fear hell, if there be no such thing?

I am very anxious, therefore, that you, my dear children, in the very morning of life, should have full and clear proof, that though *men* may lie, and cheat, and deceive each other, yet there is *One* who will not—he is "a God of truth."

1. *The manner in which God has made men, shows that he is a God of truth.*

Perhaps you may, some of you, have been told by your father how wicked it is to lie,—perhaps you may have been punished for falsehood. Why did your father do so? Because he wishes his child to hate falsehood and to love truth. That father knows he will die in a few years, and he wishes his child to think of him, to love his memory, and his character, after he is dead. But suppose the father had himself been a deceitful man and a liar, all his days. Has he taken the right way to make his child love his memory? Would a liar teach a child to love truth, and then expect him to love his father? Impossible.

Now, you all know that God has made us, and every thing else, and made us just as he pleased. Nobody directed him, nobody taught him. He could then, if he had chosen to do it, have made us very different from what we are. He could have made but one eye, or one hand, or he could have given us four feet instead of two. So he could have made us to think and feel differently if he chose; but how *has* he done?

Why, he has made us so, that if there be any thing in the world which we *despise*, it is a *liar*. We call him mean, cowardly, and vile. It is *impossible* for any man, however much he may try to do it, to love or respect a liar, or one who does not *love* the truth.

Now, God wants us to love him, and respect and esteem him; but he must have known, that, created as we are, we never *could* do it, if he be not a God of truth. If he were not a being of truth, it would be in vain to tell us to respect and love him,—we *could not do it!* Do you see the proof? It is this. If God had made us so that we could respect and love a liar, then we might have loved him, had he not been a God of truth; but as he has made us so that we love only those who love truth, he himself, making us to love him, must be a God of truth.

2. *God has forbidden deceit of all kinds*, and this shows that he is a God of truth.

Suppose a dishonest man, or a liar, reads the Bible,—can he read it with any comfort? There, you are told not to lie one to another, for all liars have their part in the lake of fire and brimstone. There, you are forbidden to deceive, though kings stand over you with drawn swords,—though prisons are your homes, and death your portion.

What multitudes of men might have been saved from persecution, if they would only deceive a little! Yet holy Daniel would not.

The three men who were put into the furnace alive, would have been spared, had they bent the knee a single moment. But they would not.

Martyrs might have saved their lives, had they been willing to nod the head, or sprinkle a little powder on the altar of an idol; but these men knew that God had forbidden all lying, and would blot their names out of the book of life if they deceived.

Suppose that one of these little boys were now in the hands of the Mohammedans, and a man was now standing over him with a sword, declaring that when five minutes were up, the little boy should die, if he did not say that he would leave Christ and become a true Mohommedan! The boy could not do it—he *could not* really believe in Mahomet. But why might he not *pretend* to do it, and thus save his life by deceiving? Because you all know, that a life on earth, in the sight of God, is of no consequence, compared with *truth*, and *sincerity*:—because you know that God has forbidden *all* falsehood, and any one who regards truth so little that he would tell a lie to save his life, is not fit for heaven. He would sell his Savior, or God the Father, to save his life, if that were necessary.

If you tell a lie about any man, or any thing, you lead others to measure that man or that thing wrong;—it is the same thing as a false measure, or a false balance, with which a merchant sells things. God abhors it and forbids it, and this proves that he is "a God of truth."

3. The third proof that God is a God of truth, is, *that he has told us of certain facts in the Bible, and everything around us shows that these are true.*

The Bible says that men are sinners now, though God at first made them holy; and is it not so,—that every man you ever saw, or heard of, is a sinner?

The Bible says that the old world became so wicked that God cut them off by a flood,—and all nations have such a story among them; and even now, we find shells, and the bones of fish, in the very top of the mountains, where they must have been left when the waters of the flood covered the mountains.

In the Bible you read that the rainbow shall be a sign that God will no more destroy the earth with a flood; and no summer goes past without your seeing this beautiful bow hanging on the dark cloud, to remind us that God is a God of truth.

He said that as long as the world shall endure, there shall be heat and cold, summer and winter; and you have all seen it is so. The long, cold icicle in the winter, and the bright rose in the summer, tell you of this truth.

He tells us that he once burned up five great and wicked cities: and there—in the land of Palestine, the dark, gloomy Dead Sea still lies, and, with a sullen roar, tells us that here is the monument of the cities, and of God's truth.

He said he would cut off all the firstborn in the land of Egypt, in a single night; and the Jews in all countries still keep the Passover, because the angel *passed over* them, when he went to destroy,—and this feast, still kept alive, tells you that God speaks the truth.

God says that he took a shepherd's boy, and raised him up to be a king; and do you not still read the sweet Psalms which David wrote?

Did not God make every thing just as he pleased? You say, "Yes." Does he not direct and order every thing just as he sees best? Some of you answer me, "Yes." Why, then, should he not tell us about every thing just as it is? He says that sin must always have misery go with it. Misery is tied to sin just as much as a shadow is to any thing which makes it. And did you ever hear of a murderer whose brow was smooth, and whose sleep was sweet? Did you ever hear of a dishonest man who was happy?

A few years ago, and there was a man who lived in a beautiful house, with beautiful furniture, and every thing around him was beautiful. One day he was in the post-office, and he saw a letter directed to the sheriff, and he went home as quick as he could, and took his gun and went out in the lot and shot himself dead! Why did he do so? Because he had built that house, and bought all those fine things, with money which he had got by lying and deceiving. Was he a happy man, who, by looking on the *outside* of a letter, would hasten away and kill himself? He knew that it had all come out, and he must go to prison; and so he shot himself, and went all bloody and guilty to God! Could he be happy?

And is not every sinner, from the smallest child here, like some of those that can hardly speak, to the vilest spirit in hell,—is not every one unhappy in proportion to his sins? This proves to you that God, who has fastened misery to sin, is "a God of truth."

4. *God shows us that he is a God of truth, by always keeping his own promises.*

We do not judge of men by what they *say* about themselves; because a rogue often says he is honest, and a coward that he has courage; but we judge by what we see men *do*. If a man *has* always kept his word, we call him a man of truth.

God once said to Abraham that he would give him a son. It seemed impossible, and the faith of Abraham was almost staggered by it, but he kept his word.

He promised to bring Israel out of Egypt, when they were sunk down as slaves. It seemed impossible; but he raised up Moses,—fed him at the very table of the king who tried to destroy Israel,—and then sent him away to be a shepherd forty years, that he might learn to be modest and humble, and then made him the leader of Israel.

He promised that the long captivity of the Jews in Babylon should end. It seemed impossible;—but Daniel was raised up to be their friend during all of it.

5. *God punishes all deceit and lying, and this shows that he is a God of truth.*

I do not mean by this that he *will* do it sometime or other, but I mean that he *has* done it—*is doing it*, and *will* do it.

Do you recollect how severely he punished Saul, the king of Israel, for lying about some cattle? 1 Sam 15.

Gehazi, the servant of the prophet Elisha, told one lie, and by a miracle he was turned into a leper the rest of his life.

And by his providence, God has so directed things, that men *must*, for the most part, speak the truth, or the whole of human society must be broken up. Even robbers must speak the truth, and be true to one another.

Did you ever hear of the three robbers in Germany, who were not true to each other? I will tell you the story. They were going to divide the things and the money which they had stolen, and then separate. Two of them sent the other into the city to buy some food, and agreed that when he got back, they would kill him, and divide all between themselves. The other one thought he would have all the goods himself, and so he put poison into the food of the other two! On his return, they suddenly fell upon him and killed him, and then sat down to eat. They ate the poison, and in a few hours they too were dead; and thus all three were found dead, because they were not true to each other. And thus it would be, through all society, if all undertook to lie and deceive.

Nothing will bring upon any body the scorn, the hatred, the contempt, and the curses of men, so quickly and surely, as to be a liar. The most wicked men in the world see and know this; and therefore, though they are vile every other way, yet they try to speak the truth.

It makes no difference whether the liar be a man, or a whole nation of men. A nation that lies and perjures itself, is near its end and its ruin. It is the law of God, unalterable too, that the man, or the number of men, who will not uphold truth, shall perish and be put out of the way. But beyond this life, in the lake of fire, will God most awfully punish *all liars*. Not *one* shall stand in heaven, and if one kind of shame and contempt is more dreadful than another, the most dreadful will be poured upon the head of the *liar*. Ah! God pursues and crushes any and all who lie and deceive, all the way through this life, and then follows them far into the eternal world, and there for ever holds them up to shame and scorn, because he is "a God of truth."

One more proof that he is a God of truth, and that is,

6. *That he has no temptation to break his word, or to deceive anyone in anything.*

Why do men break promises, and deceive, and disappoint?

Sometimes they do it because they do not know how much labour and expense it will cost to keep their word; they do not know their own weakness, nor how many difficulties they may meet with in the way.

Not so with God. He knows all that can take place, all the difficulties, before he makes a promise. He has power to bring down the highest mountain, to make the sea dry land, or to make stones into men or angels, if he needs—to keep his word.

Men sometimes feel that it is convenient to deceive,—they can make a better bargain, or they can appear better. Not so with God. He has no bargains to make, no weakness or poverty to cover up, no points to carry which need falsehood to aid him.

Men sometimes change in their views and feelings, and therefore break their promises. But with God there is no change, neither shadow of turning. He does not begin a plan today, and leave it tomorrow, because he is weary, or discouraged, or wants tools, or has some new plan come in before him.

Men have prejudices and hatreds, and sometimes try to ensnare their enemy by deceit. God does not do so. He can punish an enemy without ensnaring him; reach him without deceiving him; and deal with him without lying.

Men sometimes lie and deceive, because they want something which they cannot get. Sometimes they are hungry, and want food; sometimes their families are suffering, and they want money to buy them food; sometimes they have debts which they cannot pay; sometimes they want to save their reputation, or to gain more, or they want honors, or distinctions, or notice, which *they* cannot get, and therefore they put on, and *appear* to have and to be what they are not. How many who are poor, try to *appear* rich! How many who are ignorant, try to *appear* learned! How many who are vile, try to *appear* like good, honest people! How many try to appear generous, who are not!

It is not so with the great and glorious God. He has no wishes which his goodness, and power, and wisdom cannot meet; he has no hunger to be appeased by food;—no creatures crying for food, which he cannot feed; he wants no honors, or titles, or distinctions, which holy beings will not yield to him; no;—he is just what he *appears* to be;—will do just as he has promised; and there is not, in all the great world, or in all worlds, any thing that can tempt him not to keep his word. Ah! men may deceive and lie, and angels turn into devils; but God is true, and his word is Amen.

And now, children, I am going to stop, after having mentioned *one* single *inference*, which I wish you would remember, in addition to what I have already said. The inference is,

That God is well fitted to be the ruler of angels and of men.

Anything created must be weak. Among the most glorious angels sin was once found.

And now, suppose, at this moment, an angel in heaven is just opening his wings to fly down to this world on some errand of love. That angel cannot move without aid from God,—he cannot stand without having him to lean upon; he cannot think without help;—he cannot come and do the errand without help from God. On whom shall he lean? In whom shall he live? By whose aid shall he fly?

Ah! there is only *one* pillar in the universe that can stand up alone, and not be shaken; only *one* arm that can move itself; only *one* that can live in himself by his own power. That angel leaps up with joy, and spreads his wings, knowing that for ever and ever he will be as he now is. And how does he know it? Because he knows that God has said, "They shall not be confounded that put their trust in me," and he knows that God is "a God of truth."

Just so it is with good men on earth. They may see mountains shake and be carried away into the sea, and the nations troubled; but their song is, "The Lord is with us, the God of Jacob is our refuge—*therefore* will we not fear."

Glorious apostle Paul! stripes, and imprisonments, and sufferings, and death, awaited him, but they do not move him. "Faithful is he who hath called us, who also will do it."

Blessed martyr Stephen! the stones bruise his body, but cannot crush his spirit, nor his hopes! Why not? "I see heaven opened, and Jesus standing at the right hand of God."

Ah! I am a poor little child, says one, and when that dark cloud shall gather over me, and cover my way, and the storm shall come, shall I not fear? No, no! I hear his voice saying, "Fear not, thou worm Jacob,—I am with thee."

Yes, but waves roll over me, the deep is heaved, and the grave yawns, and death has his dart in his hand—shall I not *now* fear? No, no; I see one coming, walking on the stormy deep, and I hear his voice, "*It is I*, be not afraid,—peace, be still!"

But I must go down into the grave, so dark and cheerless! Silence is there; and the worm is there;—it is all cheerless; shall I not now be afraid? No! there is a sweet voice in the tomb, saying, "I am the resurrection and the life; he that believeth on me, though he were dead, yet shall he live, and I will raise him up at the last day."

Do I feel my own heart to be full of sin, and doubts, and darkness, and fears; and do I feel like a living man with a dead body chained to him, crying out, "Who shall deliver me from the body of this sin and death?" My heart breaks out in the song, "Thanks be unto God, through Jesus Christ, who giveth me the victory." God changes not,—is not a man that he should lie, nor the son of man that he should repent; he hath said, and his word shall stand. "Heaven and earth shall pass away, but his word shall not pass away!"

Glorious Being! make these children to love *truth*, to be *sincere* in heart,—blessed and useful while they live here on earth,—happy and peaceful when they die,—and make them, through Christ the Redeemer, to walk with the angels in light, in thine own bright presence for ever! Amen.

LECTURE 9.—GOD DOES AS HE PLEASES

HE DOETH ACCORDING TO HIS WILL IN THE ARMY OF
HEAVEN, AND AMONG THE INHABITANTS OF THE EARTH.
—Dan 4:35

Things great—Things bright—ancient—Niagara—Wise men—Death—Mind governs—Men govern cattle—why?—God's *right* to do as he pleases—A painter—West's picture—Why his property—A new island—Whose property—No creature may complain—The insect—The farmer—The rock and the sun—Why a child should obey—Our dependence on God—Pharaoh—King of Babylon—God bought us—All are sinners—How we were bought—God *uses* the right to do as he pleases—Proved by his creating—by his keeping the world—sending his Son—by every child—Story of the little girl—The inference from the story—*God's making and altering his laws*, shows that he does as he pleases—The law of the sun—of the Sabbath—of baptism—Extent of God's laws—Law of fire—of the lion—Destruction of Jerusalem—God punishes for breaking his laws just as he pleases—gives and takes away as he pleases—*One thing to be remembered*—The rosebush—The fair flower—Walking the streets—Why not envy—Story of the sick stranger—The discontented boys—Why God pleases to do as he does—What a Being is God—Conclusion.

You have seen things great,—such as the ocean, the earth on which we live, the heavens, the sun, the moon, and the stars;—but *He* who made them all, must be greater than all.

You have seen things *bright*,—such as the sunrise and early dawn,—the summer's evening sky,—the light which fills creation; but we know that *He* who made all that is beautiful, must be more glorious than all.

You have seen things *ancient,*—such as the wilderness, the solitary rock, the high mountain, and the old roaring ocean; but we know that *He* who is from eternity is more ancient than all these.

You have seen things *powerful,*—such as the cannon, the lightning which leaps from cloud to cloud, and the thunder which follows,—and you have heard of the great falls of Niagara, where the waters, from several great lakes, go thundering down more than a hundred feet; but we know that *He* who calls these his servants, is more powerful than all.

You have seen *wise* men,—men who could rear the lofty marble building,—make and navigate the great ship over the mighty waters, or, with their long telescopes, could watch and measure the heavens; but we know that *He* who created all these, must be wiser than the wisest of men.

We see men die, and see them carried to the grave;—and we know that nations have all gone down to the grave; but we know that *He* who sits in the heavens, and grows no older while nations perish, must be everlasting in all his ways.

Now, what child does not know that his *mind* governs his body; that he walks, or moves his hand, or does anything else, because his *mind* tells his body to do it? Why is this? Because the mind *thinks,* and that ought to govern the body. Do not *men* govern cattle, the horse, the ox, the cow, and all the cattle? Why do they? Because they have more *mind* than the cattle; and what has the most mind, if his feelings are right and good, ought to govern. When the angels used to come down to earth so as to be seen by men, the prophets and apostles felt like falling down before them, and letting them direct them. The angel spoke to Philip, and told him to go to the Ethiopian, Acts 8, and he went. He told Peter to dress himself and follow him, Acts 12, and Peter obeyed him at once. We always feel that a mind that is great, wise, good, and just, ought to govern. Now God is higher than all, wiser than all, stronger than all, more knowing than all, more benevolent than all,—has a nature every way more exalted, and *therefore* he has a *right to do as he pleases.*

You all know that a *man* has a right to do what he pleases with his own property.

A painter once bought a large piece of coarse cloth; he then bought some colors, and some hair pencils. He spent years over that piece of cloth, and when it was finished, it was a most beautiful picture of Christ healing the sick in the Temple at Jerusalem. It was greatly admired, and was worth many thousands of dollars. Suppose, now, another man had come in, and said that the picture was *his,* and that *he* must have the price of it, and that *he* must be called the author of it! Would not this be wrong`? You say, Yes,—the painter owned the picture. It is his, because he made it. And so it is. That painter was Benjamin West, and he gave the picture to the Hospital at Philadelphia, where it now hangs, and which brings a great deal of money to the Hospital from the visitors. He had a *right* to give it away, because it was his. He made it. But, after all, he did not *create* the cloth, nor the colors, nor the brushes, nor the hand that held the brush, nor the mind that guided the hand; and yet every body feels that it was his, and he might do with it just as he pleased. And may not God, who made all things in this world, and in all worlds, do just as he pleases with his own?

May not a man do what he pleases with his lamb, his cow, or his horse, because, though he did not create them, yet they are his? And may not God, who *did* create everything, do as he pleases?

A man may sail away on the ocean in a ship which he has bought, and discover a large and beautiful island on which nobody lives. Is it not *his*? May he not live there, and plant and reap, and own it all if he pleases? What shall we, then, say of *Him* who made all things out of nothing,— who borrowed nothing, received nothing, who was taught by no one,— who gave to every creature and to everything all that they have,—is *He* not the owner of all, and has he not a *right to do just as he pleases*?

Nothing created has any right to complain. May the cold stone in the street complain that it was not made into a diamond, and put in the crown of a king? May the worm complain that he must creep and be crushed under foot, while the elephant walks away in his wild home, free and secure in his great strength? May the little spotted insect complain because God did not make him into the eagle, to soar above the clouds, and to rise up so high that the storm cannot ruffle a feather on his bosom? No, no. Nor may the farmer complain that he must toil on his mother earth, while thousands have nothing to do but to ride out in their splendid carriages. And we who are dying men, to stay here a few days and then die, may not complain that God did not make us into angels, and let us even now be drinking of the river of life, which flows from the throne of God. He is the Creator of all, and therefore he has a *right* to do just as he pleases.

He took the materials which he had made, and a part he made into the bright sun; a part into the curious body of Adam, into which he breathed life; and a part he made into the cold rock, and put it down in the dark ground, and buried it up. Has the rock any right to complain of its Creator?

God gives to all his creatures all that they have. "His creatures all wait upon him: they gather that which he gives them: he turns away his face,—they are troubled: he taketh away their breath, they die and return to the dust." [Ps 104:27-29]

Suppose one of these children should say that he would not obey his father; that his father has no right to direct him; and yet that boy must go to his father's table for food, to his house for shelter, to him for clothing, to him for money to buy books with, and with which to pay his teachers,—would not that boy be doing very wrong? As long as he must depend on his father for every thing, may not the father direct him? You all say, "Yes." Very well. But the time will never come, in this life or the next, when any man or any creature can say to God, "*Let go thy hand, I can live without thee;*" and so long as we must thus depend upon God, he has a right to do as he pleases, and to command us just as he pleases.

Wicked men do not like to feel this dependence on God; but what can they do? Pharaoh may say, I will not obey the Lord, and may feel that his throne is so high he is independent. But no,—it was God who raised him to it, and it was God who hurled him from it. The proud king of Babylon may say, "Is not this great Babylon, which *I* have builded by the power of *my* might?" [Dan 4:30] and God will call him down and rebuke him, by saying, "God, in whose hands thy life and thy breath is, and whose are all thy ways, thou hast not glorified."

I have one more reason to mention, why God has a *right* to do with men *just as he pleases*, and that is, *he bought us.*

If a *man* buys anything, and pays for it all that it is worth, may he not do with it just as he pleases? If he buys a horse, he may keep him for the saddle, or he may put him into the carriage, or he may put him to the plough.

Now, the Bible says, "we have been *bought* with a price, not with corruptible things, as with silver and gold, but by the precious blood of the Son of God." When we were "all gone astray—had all become filthy, and there was none righteous, no, not one,"—when there was no eye to pity, and no arm to save,—when no man could redeem his brother, or give God a ransom for his own soul,—what then was our condition? Did men mourn and lament their sins, and cry to God for help? No,—they wandered, and loved to wander, just as a sheep that has run away to the mountains, loves to wander and has no desire to come back to her master, though the wolves are howling around her, and she is almost starving for food.

We were thus when Christ *died* for us,—the just for the unjust,— that he might redeem us, and bring us back to holiness and to God. He, the Son of God, came down to this world; he went about doing good,— he was taken by wicked men, and they despised him, and mocked him, and spit upon him, and struck him, and whipped him with rods on his naked back, and then they nailed him to a tree, and let him hang there till he died! And all this Christ suffered that he might buy us, and bring us near to God. And because God has thus bought us, "we are not our own,"—we are the property of God, and he has a *right* to us and over us.

I wish now to show you, children, not only that God has a *right to do as he pleases*, but also that he *uses* that right.

Can any one of these little girls tell me how long, or about how long it is, since God made this world and all that is in it?

"Nearly six thousand years," says one fine, clear voice. Very well. But when God began to make things, before he had made any one thing, who was there to advise him, or to command him, or to ask him to make them? You say again, "Nobody." Very well. Then God was free to make things or not to make them, to make more of them or less, and to do just as he pleased in regard to creating all things,—was he not?

You say that God has *kept* this world, and fed all his creatures here, nearly six thousand years;—do any of these little boys know how much longer the world will last, and the sun shine upon it? "No, sir." Then it is for *God* to say how much longer the world will last, and he may destroy it just when he pleases.

How long ago is it since Christ was on earth? Can any one tell? "Almost two thousand years." Very well. But why did he not come sooner? Because God did not choose to send him sooner. Why did he not wait and come *now*, so that *we* could see him? Because God was pleased to send him then.

I see these children have all got two hands, and two eyes, and two feet each. I do not see a single lame or blind child here. But was it not for God to say whether you should be born with all your limbs perfect, or not?

In one of our asylums is a sweet little girl, about eight years old when she went there. She is entirely *blind*, and *deaf*, and *dumb*, and almost unable to smell any thing. Poor child! How dark must the world be, when she never saw a single thing in her life! How lonely must it be, when she never spoke a word to any human being, and never heard a single voice or noise! And yet she is a sweet child, and with her fingers they teach her to read and write. But the soul is shut up in that dark house, and will never be able to look out, nor to speak out, nor to hear, till it leaves the body at death!

Now, I ask these children, if we ought not to thank God for giving us eyes, and ears, and a tongue, which we can use, so that we can see, and hear, and speak? Ought we not to be *thankful?* "Yes, yes," you all say. Well, this thanking God is the same thing as saying that he had a *right* to make us all, just as he did make that poor child. Who but God made her just as she is? And why did he do so? "Even so, Father, for so it seemeth good in thy sight."

He may give property, or health, or life, and he may take them away again, just as he pleases, and he does do so. He makes one a king's son, and another the son of a chimney-sweep; he gives one health, and from another takes it away, as he pleases.

God uses his right to do as he pleases, *in making and altering his own laws.*

When the sun was created, God gave him a law that he should rise and set every day at a certain moment; and yet on a certain time he altered the law, and at the command of Joshua, the sun stood still in the heavens.

When he made the great seas, he gave them laws, and said, "Hitherto shall ye come, and here shall your proud waves be stayed;" and yet when he wanted to drown the world, he broke up the foundations of the deep, and made the waters cover the whole earth.

When he had finished creating the heavens and the world, he commanded that the seventh day should be kept holy; and yet Christ, who is Lord of the Sabbath, went about on that day preaching and healing the sick. God might have selected any other day, and have made it the Sabbath, or he might, as he did, after Christ had gone to heaven, have altered it, and then taken the *first* day of the week, which is our Sabbath.

God made a law that whosoever should kill a man, should lose his life; and yet he repealed the law himself, long enough to command that Cain should not be killed, though he was a murderer; and to command Abraham to slay his own son. He gives, and changes, and alters his laws, just as he pleases. He once commanded that little children should be circumcised, to show that they belonged to his people; *now*, he has altered that, and we use baptism by water for the same purpose.

The laws of God, too, are very wide. One city, or one country, cannot make laws for another; but God makes laws that reach all cities, and nations, and ages, angels and men; his laws reach the smallest insect that creeps on the leaf of the tree, and the loftiest seraph in heaven. The laws of men reach only the body,—only one half of a man, and that the poorest half. You may not do this or that; but you may *think* it, and *wish* it, and *plan* it; but the laws of God as really and as fully bind every thought and feeling, as they do any great actions, even such as kings do, when they act for a nation.

It is a law of God that fire shall burn; but he can so alter that law, that three men can walk in the furnace heated seven times hotter than usual, and yet they shall not be hurt, Dan 3.

It is another law, that a hungry lion shall kill and eat; and yet he can alter the law so that the holy man shall sleep all night in a den full of lions, and they shall not hurt him.

Did these children, any of them, ever read the history of the destruction of Jerusalem, under Titus, the Roman warrior? If you have not, or have not lately, I wish you would do it. Josephus, the Jew, wrote the whole story. There you will see this remarkable thing;—that on the coming of Christ, God would alter and do away all the laws and customs which he had given the Jews. He had told them in Daniel, that when Christ came, they were no longer to sacrifice beasts every day in the temple; but the Jews were not willing to have God alter this law and this custom, and so he buried their altar and their sacrifices all under the ruins of the temple, and the poor Jews were scattered all over the earth, and were compelled to let God alter these laws, and take away the daily sacrifices, and do as he pleased.

And when God punishes men for breaking his laws, how terribly he does it,—and in what different ways! Sometimes he comes in the famine, and a nation melts away in feebleness. Sometimes he walks on the wings of the wind, or rides the hurricane, and then what can stand before him? Sometimes he shakes the earth, and whole cities fall down in a few moments. "He sits king upon the waters," says the psalmist; and with those great waters, when they are calm and still, he reflects the bright heavens as if they were a great looking-glass; or he heaves them with the winds, and tosses the ship as if she were a feather; or with these waters he buries Egypt, or drowns the world.

He gives, or takes away, or withholds from his creatures, just what and how he pleases. Some are born black, some white, some in heathen lands, some in Christian, some rich, and some poor, some to be well, and some to be sick all their days, because God does as he pleases.

And now, my dear children, there is one thing which I want you to remember and keep in mind.

1. *That you must not envy anybody what they have and you have not, because God can do no wrong.*

Suppose you have a beautiful rosebush in a little flowerpot. You go to it, and you pluck one, and wear it in your bosom, or you give it to your friend. Why should you not,—is it not your own, and may you not do what you please with it? Thus God comes into a family, and perhaps takes your little sister away by death, the fairest flower among you all. He puts it in the grave, and hides it there. But he does no wrong.

The owner goes to his flock and selects a lamb. He takes *which* he pleases, and he gives it away, or sells it, or uses it for food. May he not do with it as he pleases?

Thus God gives one thing to one man, and another to a second. I walk out in the streets sometimes, and I see splendid carriages, with costly horses, servants to drive, and to wait upon the owner; I see some beautiful houses with rich furniture, and more wealth than the owner knows what to do with; but may I, because I am a poor man, envy these men, and feel that God ought to have made me rich? No, no. It is as wrong for me to envy the rich man who rides, as to despise the servant who drives, or who washes and scrubs the doorsteps. God has a right to give riches where he pleases, and he does no one any wrong. So when he gives one little boy fine health, and fine limbs, so that he can run and jump about, and another is feeble, and sickly, and lame, and shut up at home, the sick child may not envy, for God has done it; and we know that what he does is right.

A poor sick man once came along, and told a gentleman whom he met that he was a stranger, and sick. The man was kind, and felt for the stranger; but he had a large family, and knew not how to take him in. At last he recollected that the little boys had a room in which they played. So he put up a bed in that room, and put the sick man there, and called a physician. The doctor said the man was very sick, and that he had the smallpox.

Now the father did not wish to tell his boys that the sick man was there, lest it should alarm the neighbors too much. So he told the boys that *they must not go to their playroom till he again gave them permission.* The boys felt disappointed and very angry towards their father. They saw him go into the room, and saw their mother, and they *envied* them, and felt that their father was doing them wrong by not letting them go there, or at least by not telling them the reason *why* they could not. But when the man got well, and they saw how pale he looked, and how thankful he felt, and that nobody had been alarmed and nobody hurt, they saw that their father did right, and they were wrong.

Just so it is with our heavenly Father. He does just as he pleases; i.e. he does just as he sees best, without asking any one, and without telling us the reason why he does this or that thing. For every thing which he does, he has reasons, wise and holy and good;—but he sees it is not best for us to know them, and so he tells us to believe he knows best, and to rejoice that he is such a God. In heaven they all feel so, and cry, "Just and true are all thy ways, thou King of saints." You pray to God, and you speak to one who can speak and it is done, command and it stands fast; who ruleth in the army in heaven, and among the inhabitants of the earth. He can do all things that are for the best,—he can correct you with afflictions, and comfort you with the oil of joy. What a Being! No cedar of Lebanon is so tall that his lightning cannot reach it; no hell is so deep that his eye cannot pierce it; no spirit so mighty that he cannot control it; no courage so strong that he cannot quail it. Oh! the mountains shall depart, and the hills shall be removed, but his kindness shall never depart from his people, though his wrath shall burn to the lowest hell. Let us all rise up and say, "The Lord reigneth, let the earth rejoice." Amen.

LECTURE 10.—GOD IS HOLY

**YE SHALL BE HOLY;
FOR I THE LORD YOUR GOD AM HOLY.**—Lev 19:2

Saying of Plutarch—A father's likeness—The most beautiful part of man—The most beautiful part of God—Giving a *pledge*—God's pledge—What makes a church solemn—How we can copy God—What God would be if not holy—What does the holiness of God mean—*The first thing*—Pure gold—White garment—2. *God hates some things and loves others*—3. *God by nature holy*—4. *God hates sin wherever seen*—The weeds—The cancer—Drunkenness—Moses—Uzzah—David—Jonah—Peter—*First proof that God is holy*—The jarring instrument—The leaky ship—the imperfect watch—Broken jar—The argument—*Second proof that God is holy*—Bowl full of sunbeams—The fountain—God's laws strict—Human laws very different—The laws of men—God's laws do not change—How the Jews taught—The sacrifices—God punishes breaking his laws—*Third proof that God is holy*—Sending his Son—Bruising his Son—Christ's great sufferings—God of the Bible different from other gods—What gods men have made—Heathen gods—Impure gods—Wicked men—What a god would such men make—A caution—Two men on an island—Who are wrong, and why?—Conclusion.

There was a man who lived many hundreds of years ago, by the name of *Plutarch*. He was a writer of history. He used to say that a man who denied there was any such person as Plutarch, did him less injury than if he had said that Plutarch was a debauched and vicious person. I suppose this was true. And I suppose that the man who should deny that there is any God, would do less hurt than the man who should teach that God is not a holy being.

Suppose one of these children, who has a father whom he loves very much, were now just going to get a likeness of his father painted. What part of your father should you wish painted? You answer, "The *face.*" What part would you wish painted the best,—what part have most pains taken with it? You answer again, "The face." And why the face? Because it is the most beautiful and noble part of man. And why? Because it shows the mind, the feelings, the soul within, more clearly than any other part. And suppose the painter could paint the *mind* of your father just as he can the face, would you not wish him to do it? And if you were to be wounded, and have great and ugly scars left, would you not hate to have the wounds come on the *face* more than any where else? The reason is, the face is the most beautiful part of man, and *therefore* we do not like to have it scarred, and therefore we want the painter to take special pains with it.

Now, *holiness* is the most beautiful part of the character of God, and therefore the writers of the Bible take great pains to make us see this part. They take us up into heaven, and show us the angels covering their faces with their wings, and crying one to another, and saying, "Holy, holy, holy, is the Lord God of hosts." [Isa 6:3] What a lofty song is that! They cover their faces and their feet, as if they were ashamed to be seen in the presence of a God so holy.

Suppose, now, a man wanted to give to another the highest *pledge* in his power. What would be that pledge? What was it in the case of Judah, when he made that most beautiful plea before his brother Joseph, when entreating him to send Benjamin up to his aged father? He gives Joseph a *pledge*, and the highest in his power; and what is that? Is it money? No. Is it one of his arms, or an eye? No. But it is his *life*. This was the highest pledge in his power. So when the great God would make his people feel safe and happy, even when in trouble, he makes them promises; and lest these should not be enough, he gives them a *pledge*, and that pledge is his *holiness*. He swears by his holiness that he will do so and so; and he swears by this oftener than by any other part of his character.

What makes a *church* a more solemn place than any other house? Is it because God here shows that he knows all things, or that he is present every where, or that he is powerful, more than he shows these in other places? No: that is not it. But God shows his *holiness* in his church more than any where else, and that makes it the gate of heaven, that makes us feel "holiness becometh thine house, O Lord, for ever."

You know we are directed to copy God, and be like him. What is it we are to copy? Not his knowledge,—for we cannot know all things as he does. Not his power, for he can do all things, and "we are crushed before the moth." Not his years, for he is everlasting, and we are of yesterday. What *are* we to copy? It is his *holiness*,—we are to be holy, because he is holy.

You see by all these remarks that holiness is something which God values, whether we do or not. Take away the *strength* of God, and he would be weak like a man. Take away his *knowledge*, and he would be ignorant, and we could not trust him. Take away his *wisdom*, and he would be very imperfect. Take away his *eye* that sees everything, and he would be feeble. But take away his *holiness*, and he would be a devil! Let him have almighty power, and everlasting years, and his great knowledge, without holiness, and every created being would wish to fly from him in awful terror. The very thought of such a God is dreadful.

When I say that to be *holy* means *to be good and to love to do good*, I suppose you will all understand what I mean. But this is such holiness as good men and good angels have. The holiness of God means,

1. *That he is free from all sin.*

When we call a man holy, we mean one who has more holy feelings than wicked; who is sorry when he sins, and longs to be free from all sin. But when we say that God is holy, we mean that he never had, and never can have, any sin, just as pure gold is free from lead, and silver, and dirt, and every thing else. Just as we say a garment is pure and unspotted, when there is no stain and no spot on any part of it. But how easy it is to mix something else with the gold, and make it impure! The gold does not *hate* and reject the dirt which may be mixed with it. How easy to soil and spot the pure white garment! The garment does not feel hatred towards dirt. To say, then, that God is free from all sin, is not saying enough. For,

2. *It means that he hates sin, and loves holiness.*

Whenever God sees an honest man and a dishonest man, he at once loves the one and hates the other. When he hears one man uttering a truth and another man a lie, he loves the one and hates the other. Light and darkness cannot exist in the same place at the same moment. If it be midday, darkness must flee away. So if God be holy, he must and does love all that is good, and hate all that is evil.

3. *Holiness is a part of his very nature.*

God can make a world or not, just as he pleases; but if he make it, because his very nature is good, the world must also be good. He can speak from heaven to men or not, just as he pleases; but if he does speak, he cannot speak a lie. He cannot deceive, and yet be God. Truth and holiness are a part of himself. A man may speak or not, just as he please; but if he speaks, he must use the tongue. There is no other way for him to do. So God may permit men to sin or not, just as he pleases; but if they do sin, it is impossible for him not to hate their sins. He chooses holiness, he loves it, and he hates sin of his own choice, and we praise him for it.

4. *The holiness of God means that he hates sin in all places, wherever he sees it.*

A crop of rank weeds is an unpleasant sight. If in a garden, it is still more unpleasant. But suppose you have a choice flower-garden, are not these weeds more unpleasant there than any where else?

You know that a cancer is one of the most disagreeable of all evils. You hate to see it any where; but if it fasten on your breast near the heart, or on your face, is it not still more disagreeable and hateful? So it is with sin, in the view of God.

Heaven is the garden of the Lord. And when sin entered it, and some of the bright angels sinned, he was peculiarly displeased, and turned them all out of heaven, and cast them down to hell. The cancer was too near the seat of life.

Who does not loathe drunkenness? And yet how much more unpleasant is it, when it comes into your own family, and your father, or mother, or brother, becomes a drunkard!

So when God sees sin in his own family, among good people, he hates it as much, or more, than any where else.

Moses was impatient and sinned once; and God punished him by not allowing him to enter the land of promise.

David sinned greatly, and God punished him by sending deaths, and family quarrels, and troubles into his house all the days of his life.

Uzzah was going beside the cart on which the ark of God rested, and seeing it shaken, he ran and put out his hand to make it steady. This was the business of the Levite, and every body else was forbidden to go near it; and so God struck him dead for breaking his commands.

Jonah was a prophet of the Lord; and when God sent him on a mission to a great heathen city, he did not like to go, and so he tried to run away. You know the rest. God sent the great storm and the mighty wind, and then the great fish after him, to punish him for his sins. And when Peter sinned and tried to oppose Christ as he went to Jerusalem, the Saviour rebukes him and calls him "Satan!" [Matt 16:23; Mark 8:33; Luke 4:8] God hates sin among his people as much as any where else, and more too. And this is one reason why he often afflicts and punishes good people, while the wicked escape.

Shall I now tell you a few things which show that God is *holy*? Will you try to understand and remember the *proofs* that he is holy?

1. *He would not have created angels and men holy at first, unless he had been holy.*

If a man loved sweet music, and were making a curious instrument of music, would he make it so that it would jar, and a part of the notes be right, and a part wrong? And could he say that this is "a very good" instrument? A part of the angels are holy, and a part have become sinners. They jar in their feelings, like the jarring strings of a harp. Were they created so? No. All was "very good" then in the eyes of the Lord. Those men who are in heaven now are all holy; the spirits of just men made perfect: but most men who are on earth are all sinful. Were they created so unlike? No. Adam was created holy, in the image and likeness of God. Suppose a merchant should send a ship to sea which he knew was leaking, and had leaked ever since it was built, could he blame the captain if he never reached home again with his goods? Suppose a watchmaker puts a watch together when he knows that the first great wheel is wrong,—is made wrong,—can he blame all the rest of the wheels for going wrong, or can he blame the man who buys it, for not knowing the time of day? A man commits a jar of liquid to you, and tells you to keep it safely, because the liquid in it is exceedingly valuable. Can he blame you for not keeping it safe, when he knows the jar is cracked, and has been ever since it was made? No. In all such cases, we are sure there is no blame. But now, God commands all angels and all men to be holy; but if they had been *created* unholy at first, they would not have been to blame for not being holy. He must, then, have made them holy at first; and he must have made them so as to please himself best; and if making them holy pleased himself, it proves that *he is holy.*

2. *The laws of God prove that he is holy.*

If we could make a cup so curious that we could catch it full of sunbeams, just as we could of water when it rains, and if there was not one of these beams of light which was not pure and white and beautiful, we should know that the sun, which poured them out, must be pure,— should we not?

If you dip from a little stream a glass of pure, sweet water, you know that the fountain which sent it out must be pure. Now if all that comes from God is holy and pure, we know that *he* must be so also. Is there any sin which his laws allow? Where is the thief, the robber, or the murderer, who could say that God's laws allow him to do so? Who ever had an angry, jealous, envious feeling in the heart, and could say that God allows it? Who ever spoke an unholy or impure word, or had such a feeling, and felt that God permits this, and approves of it?

How very different are the laws of men! They command you not to do this or that—not because the thing is wrong in itself, but because it hurts human society. Human laws never punish theft or adultery as crimes in themselves, but only as hurtful to other men. They do not punish or forbid them because they hurt the *doer*, but because they hurt others. But God's laws forbid and punish the crime for itself, and because it hurts the doer. Thus God will punish the attempt, the desire, and the wish to do wrong, because it hurts the sinner himself. It would be foolish in men to make laws by which to reach and punish opinions or feelings, because such laws could never be executed. But the laws of God are so holy, that they reach the heart as well as the hand. Men want you should keep the porch and the parlour of the house clean; but God will allow of no dirt in the secret closet. Men want you should have the outside of the cup clean and bright; but God tells us the inside must be clean also.

When you are under human laws, you find that they change and are altered from time to time; but the great law of God, which is holy, can never alter. As long as God is worthy of the highest and best love of angels and of men, so long will he command them to love him—and that will be to eternal ages.

You know that God taught the Jews that he is holy in different ways. By the morning and evening sacrifice, when the cattle were slain, and their blood poured out like water around the altar, the Jew was taught that God is holy, and that the sinner, like himself, deserved to be slain just as the victims were. The swine wallows in the mire and dirt, and the Jew was forbidden to eat the swine, because God would teach him, that all that is filthy and vile is hated by himself.

God is holy; and when his holy laws are broken, what does he do? He turns angels out of heaven, and sends them to hell, without any hope of pardon;—he cursed man and the woman in the earth; he curses the very instruments of sin. The serpent must creep on his belly, eat his food in the dirt, and be hated by men. The gold and silver which the wicked Canaanites had used, must all be cursed, and none of it brought into the camp of Israel, Deut 20 The sons of Aaron use strange or forbidden fire, and they are consumed in death; and the very earth on which we tread is cursed, so that the brier, the thorn, the storm, and the pestilence, have their home in every part of the world.

3. *The death of Jesus Christ proves that God is holy.*

Christ came from the bosom of God, his Father. "He knew no sin," and was so holy and so good, that the Father was ever well pleased with him. Christ, too, was the Creator of all things, and was from eternity God's only Son. He came into this world to suffer instead of men,—"he died for us," and God treated him as if he were a sinner, and were to be punished as a sinner. How did he treat him? He sent him into the world poor. He lay in a manger. He was despised by men, and hated all his life. When he rode once, he was so poor, that his friends had to borrow an ass for him; so poor, that he had no place for his head to rest in. When he went to pray in a garden alone, God treated him as if he were a sinner, and he was in great horror and agony, and great drops of blood fell from him to the ground. Wicked men took him, and mocked him, and spit on him, and struck him, and then hung him up by driving great nails through his hands and his feet; but this was not the worst of it. When he hung on the cross in awful pain, God still left him, as a man would turn away from a son whom he had determined to treat as an enemy. Then did the dear Saviour cry, "My God, my God, why hast thou forsaken me?" [Matt 27:46; Mark 15:34] Thus God *bruised* his only Son, as a man would bruise a poisonous serpent. Why did he thus treat his Son?

Because Christ came to take the place of sinners, and he was thus bruised for *our* iniquities, and by his stripes *we* are healed. God is so holy, that when he comes to punish sin, his sword falls with such weight, that if his own Son stands to take the place of sinners, he is crushed and killed. How much he suffered we can never know, because we can never know how much the Son of God could endure; but we do know that he suffered so that he cried out in agony, "My Father, if it be possible, let this cup pass from me."

How very different is the God of the Bible, from any god which we would ever think of!

Holiness is the beautiful garment in which God is dressed, and which he esteems beyond all other dresses. But do *men* feel a great desire to be holy? Do they esteem it the most beautiful part of the human character? Oh, no! They shun it; they dislike it; they despise it! When men write poetry about God, they speak of his power, his greatness, and goodness,—but very seldom about his holiness. Do you know why? Are they likely to love that in God which they do not love in themselves?

Men have sometimes made gods for themselves, and what kind of gods have they made? They made, of course, just such gods as they chose. They made a god whom they called Vulcan, because he could work iron by fire; another whom they called Æsculapius, because he could cure diseases by medicines; another was Bacchus, who taught them how to make wine; Hercules, because he had great strength; Mercury, because he was full of cunning; and Jupiter, because he was so powerful. But, among them all, they never thought of making a single god who was holy! They took all the other parts of God's character, and gave them to their gods, but because they left out *holiness*, their gods were all great and impure monsters, and the holy God frowned upon all such things as objects to be worshipped.

Men once used to make their gods love the very vices and sins which they themselves loved; and so now, men are apt to think that the God of heaven is very much like themselves, and that he cares but little more about purity and holiness than they do themselves.

You know, too, that some men who are very wicked, take a great pride in being wicked. They are cunning and sharp in bargains, and are proud of it. A Sabbath-breaker is proud of his boldness in sin; a warrior is proud of the number of men whom he kills; and some are proud that they can drink more, or swear more, or sin bolder, than other men! Suppose now, that God had just such a character as these men,—what a horrible being would he be! There is not a spirit in the world of darkness who is so vile! And are *men* doing right to have a character which would make God worse than a devil, if he had it? I ask you.

Children, you will often be tempted to sin and do wrong towards men and towards God; but I beg that you will not despise the holiness and the purity of God. It is a glorious part of his character. Suppose he were to create two men, and place them alone on a beautiful island, and tell them that they might do, and act, and feel just as they pleased, and he would never call them to an account, and never punish them, do what they might. One of these men says he will curse, and swear, and steal, and murder his best friend, if he can get any thing by it. The other says that he will not do so. He will be honest and kind, and do to all just as he would like to have them do to him. Which of these men would you respect, and which would you dislike? And suppose God should say that he did not care, and would treat them both alike, would you love and respect such a God? Oh, no! God is holy, and he ought to be, and we could not love him if he were not.

They are wrong, then—who despise holiness, and keep it out of their own hearts; for they shut out the brightest part of the character of the great and blessed God. All sin banishes holiness from the heart. Be afraid to sin.

They are wrong, who, because they see much sin in the world, charge God with it, as Adam did. God hates all sin.

They are wrong, who think they love to have God holy, but who do not love to have his people holy, and despise them if they are.

They are wrong, who think they can and shall go to heaven just as they are, in all their sins, without religion, and without holiness. They forget that God has told them to be holy, and has said that "without holiness no man shall see the Lord," to enjoy him in his blessed kingdom. And to this let us all say, Amen.

LECTURE 11.—GOD IS GOOD

OH HOW GREAT IS THY GOODNESS—
BEFORE THE SONS OF MEN!
—Ps 31:19

A visitor—Paul and Barnabas—The sun—Meaning of *goodness*—The oceans—The river—The little channels—The flower—Sheep and lamb—*First thing that shows God to be good*—A jewel—A palace—The king's servants—The curious inhabitant—The soul will not die—and why—The abode of man—Adam and the creatures—The furniture of the dwelling—Wonderful provisions—*Second thing showing that God is good*—The sick father—The great mercy—God's distinguishing goodness—The captive—How the world redeemed—The Redeemer—The beautiful death—Pale corpse—*Third thing that shows God to be good*—Wicked men—Human society preserved—A look into the church—A sinner redeemed—Prayer answered—Goodness of God not to be despised—Don't complain of your lot—Not to be proud—God's great care and goodness—Must imitate God's goodness—God to be trusted—Parting words to the little reader.

Suppose a man were now to go to a heathen people who never had heard of the Bible, and should have power to heal the sick, give sight to a blind man, hearing to a deaf man; what would the people think? They would say that a God has come among us,—for none but a God *could* do such things, or if he *could*, none but a God *would*; and they would say so, because all people think *that God must be good.*

So when Paul and Barnabas went to the city of Lystra, where they healed a poor cripple, the whole city was moved, and came out and wanted to worship them as gods, for having done so good a work.

The sun, as you know, sends down his warm and cheering beams, and this makes the summer, and the harvest, and the fruits of the earth; and because the sun does this, many nations worship him as a god. They think that what does so much good must be a god.

Do these children know what *goodness* is? It is to be holy in one's own heart and feelings, and to be doing good to others; so that all that a good man does, is only his goodness acted out. If he labours for his family, it is his goodness providing for their wants; if he teaches them, it is his goodness benefiting their minds.

You know there is a great mass of waters covering the larger part of the earth. These are all *one* great body of water, though called by different names. Thus, a part of them we call the Pacific Ocean,—a part the Atlantic, and a part the Indian Ocean;—a part the Mediterranean, a part the Black, and a part the Caspian Sea,—yet they are only one great body of waters. Just so we talk about the different parts of God's character, though the word *goodness* embraces the whole.

See now if you cannot understand me. May not a river have little channels dug here and there where its waters may run, and though these channels may have different names, yet does not the river supply them all, and are they any thing but parts of the great river? We see God making men happy who deserve it not, and we call this *grace*; we see him do this when they deserve to be punished, and we call this *mercy*; we see him bearing with wicked men and not killing them, and we call it *patience*; we see him keeping his promises, though men break theirs to him and tempt him, and we call this *truth*; we see him punish the wicked so that others may be afraid to sin, and we call this *justice*. But these are all only different ways in which he shows his goodness.

You have seen a flower when it had done blossoming. How carefully it shuts its seeds up in the little pod! But when the time comes, it drops the seed and cares no more about it. They call the flower *beautiful*, but it cannot be called *good*.

You have seen the sheep take care of her lamb for some months; the moment the lamb is grown up, the mother forgets it, and cares no more about it. She cannot be said to have goodness.

But a father may have goodness; and therefore he takes care of his child as long as he lives; and when he dies, he even then loves him, and tries to do something more to make him happy. As long as he can, he is doing good to his child. But God is so good that he will be doing good to his people for ever and ever; for all that is good in heaven, upon earth, or in the seas, comes from him.

Shall I now tell you of *three* things which show God to be good?

1. *His goodness is to be seen in his creating what he has.*

Suppose you had a jewel, the brightest and the costliest ever worn by a king, would you not wish a suitable box to put it in? Ought it not to have such a box?

Suppose you were going to build a palace for a king, would you not wish to make one of great beauty and convenience?

The soul is such a jewel, and God built the body in which to keep it! And is it not a wonderful and a beautiful cabinet?

The soul is king over all creatures on earth, and is not the body the palace in which the king lives? And how good was God to make it just as he has! with just such servants as were needed; such as feet to carry it about. Does the inhabitant within wish to communicate thought? The tongue is the servant to do it. Does it wish to receive information? The ear is the servant to bring it. Does it wish to examine for itself? The eye will wait upon it, and show it all it wishes to see. And all this body, so curiously made, was built of a little dust of the ground. Half way between angels and animals, man seems to be the connecting link. His soul is like that of an angel, and his body a tabernacle of clay. Wonderful goodness indeed!

But just go within the house! What an inhabitant is there! Ah! there is a spirit in the house of clay, that is able to govern, and manage, and give names to all the cattle; that can manage the ship, that can measure the heavens, that can build up or destroy cities and kingdoms,—a spirit that can glance in an instant from here to India, or from here to the highest heavens. Other parts of God's works show great goodness; but no where has he written it in lines so clear and deep as on the soul of man.

All things that we see around us will perish and be no more; but God made the soul of man in his own image and likeness,—stamping his image upon it as a seal is stamped on wax,—and therefore the soul will live for ever.

This world was made for men. Angels do not live here, and have no inheritance here. What a wonderful inheritance has man! The grass and the flower of the field, the tree and the fruits, the tame cattle and the wild, are all his, and God has delivered them all into his hand. When he blessed Jacob for his piety, he blessed his cattle for his sake; and when he spared the dwellers in Nineveh because they repented of their sins, he had pity on their cattle also.

What a joyous morning was that when all the beasts and the birds came round Adam, their master, to receive their names! The bird hears her name, and claps her wings for joy, and hastens to the tree to pour out her song. The horse receives his name, and bounds away in his strength. The lion hears his, and away he bounds, not to howl out his anger, but to respect and obey Adam his king.

The earth is the home, the habitation of man; and how curiously is the great house furnished! The sun hangs up for ever, to give his light. The moon, to take her turn. The bright and spangled heavens, to look down in their glory and beauty. The green carpet which is spread over the earth, to be pleasant and delightful to the eye.

Does man want wood or water? They are all ready for him. Does he want tools? Let him go to the mountain and take the iron and make them. Does he want silver or gold? Let him go to the mine, and he shall find it safely laid up in the bowels of the earth. Does he want food? The valleys will give him grain, the air will give him birds, and the great waters are all his fishing places. Does he want clothing? The sheep bears it on her back, or the cotton-plant will raise it, or the little silkworm is all ready to spin it for him. Does he want music? The sweet birds will sing for him. Does he want sweet smells? The flowers shall open their sweets for him. Does he want beauty? The rose shall blush for him. Sweets does he want? The little bee shall toil for him from the dawn to the evening. Warmth does he want? The beaver and the seal will yield up their lives to supply him. Light does he need? The great whales in the far-off ocean will lay down their lives for his service. Luxuries does he want? The ocean and the tides and the winds shall all wait on him, and the ship shall go and return in safety. Say, can you think of any thing which this great house—the world, is not furnished with?

2. *The goodness of God is seen in his redeeming us.*

When God told the grass to grow, and the waters to hasten away, that the dry land might appear, these did not feel unwilling to obey. But when he speaks to us, and tells us to be good, we feel unwilling, and his word does not make us obey. He can speak and call to the light, and it will come to him; but it cost the blood of his own dear Son to make any man come to him.

Suppose you knew that a physician lived on the top of a very high and very steep mountain who can cure almost any sickness. You have a father who is sick, feeble, lame, deaf, and blind, and you have nobody to help you,—could you ever get him up the mountain to the physician? No, never. And suppose the physician hears that you have such a sick father, and he himself comes down, and in his own arms carries him up carefully, and there takes care of him and cures him. Does he not show great kindness and goodness?

Just so Christ knew that we never should return to God, and would never want to, and so he came down into this world, and was here put to death, that he might buy us from being punished as we deserved.

If all the angels that live in heaven were to come down to this world, there is not one of them who could say that God has shown him such goodness as he has shown to the poorest saint. Christ never died for angels, and so they never cry, "Thou hast redeemed us." Could all the wicked spirits in hell now lift up their voices and tell their hopes, there is not one of them who could hope that his soul will ever be saved. Christ never died for them. They were the firstborn creatures of God, and we the younger; yet God sent his Son to save us. Why did he not save them? They had more strength than we, and could serve him better. They had stronger voices, and could praise him louder. They had greater minds than ours, and could see and feel the greatness of salvation more than we can. They were more beautiful than we were, and yet they were not saved. What goodness in God was this towards us! Ah! God punished the first sinners, who were sons of light, and who stood near his throne, most awfully; but for us, he said, "Let him not go down to the pit,—I have found a ransom." "Behold, the Lion of the tribe of Judah hath prevailed to loose the seals, and to open the book"—the book that sealed our ruin for ever, without Christ.

Suppose a man wished to buy the life of a poor prisoner who was condemned to death, and should offer a piece of solid gold as large as a great church, would you not think he pitied the poor prisoner?

But if God had given a piece of gold as large as this world, and a million of such worlds, it would have been nothing to what he did give, to save us. If he had sent the holy and lofty angels down to earth, and they had all come, and all been put to death, it would have been nothing to what he did give; for Christ, his Son, is the Creator of angels, and could have made millions more. But when God sent his Son, he sent one who was as old as himself, who was as great as himself, who can do all that he himself can do, and who is as dear as himself. It was God's giving himself to be mocked of men, and cursed by men, and then hung up to die like a guilty slave. Who mourns like him who has lost an only son? Who would not give his property, his character, every thing he had on earth, to save the life of his son? But God loved his Son more than all things besides,—and yet he was so good, that he sent the blessed Redeemer into this world to save it by shedding his own blood!

And how easy now to find the way of life! The mere child, only a little more than four years old, has been known to love the Saviour, to rely on him, and to die in peace and joy. I have such a case now in my mind. She was a sweet child; and for some time before she was taken sick, she felt that she was a sinner, and that she needed the Saviour for her friend. Day after day would she go to her little room, and kneel down and pray with tears that God would forgive her sins, and not take her out of the world "before her new heart had come to her." When she was taken sick, she was soon told that she must die. She begged her father not to weep, for she was going to her dear Saviour. She heard the Scriptures read, she heard her father pray, and with a sweet smile stretched out her little hands to bid her father and mother farewell, and closed her bright eyes in death while repeating that beautiful hymn,

> "Jesus can make the dying bed
> As soft as downy pillows are!

Her poor pale body was left, but her glorious spirit went up to God! Ah! is not God very good, who has given us the gospel so plain, that such a babe could thus be ripened for heaven?

3. *God's government shows his goodness.*

The psalmist seemed to wonder when he said, "O Lord, thou preservest man and beast!" The mighty whale that swims among the great mountains of ice in the ocean, and the smallest little creeper that ever moved its legs, are alike kept and fed by God. Why does God keep and feed so many birds, and beasts, and fishes, and little insects? What good can they do to him? And why should he be so careful as to write the history of every one, and tell the sparrow where to die, and notice the hair that drops from the head? Because he is good, and loves to make even the smallest worm happy.

You know, too, that some men are very wicked; they never thank God for his mercies, and never ask him to do them good. They abuse all that he gives them. He gives them money, and they abuse and waste it. He gives them health, and they abuse that; their bodies and their souls they abuse. He gives them the Sabbath, and the Bible, and his Son, and his Holy Spirit, and they waste and abuse all. Yet he takes care of these wicked people. He feeds them, clothes them, keeps them in life, and is all the time doing them good. Who but God would do good to such?

Why do men have laws, and courts, and jails, and prisons? Because God has commanded them to do so. And why has he? Because he knew that men would be happier to live in society together; and therefore he makes every man feel that if he breaks human laws, he sins against God.

Why are men willing to give their money to build hospitals, and schoolhouses, and churches, to light and pave the streets of cities? Because God has made them *inclined* to do what will be for the public good, and thus make it more pleasant to live together. Do not all honest men love that city best, where the police is most active and awake? Does it not show great goodness in God in so moving and inclining men, that they want the laws obeyed, and the crimes punished, and the good of the whole of society taken care of?

But let us look into the church. There, in the further corner of the building, sits a poor man, who, a few years ago, was a drunkard and a sabbath-breaker; he abused his wife and his children. He was a poor, miserable creature, and all men despised him. But God did not. God sent his Spirit, and made him a humble Christian. He now prays night and morning,—his wife is happy,—his children are at school, and are happy. He is now well-dressed, and is respected. It was God's goodness that took that miserable soul, and saved him, and is now preparing him for heaven. Did you ever read the account of the poor thief who died with Christ, and whom Christ saved in that awful hour? Of Saul the persecutor, whom God converted, and made an apostle? Ah! God saves not only the sinner, the poor, the guilty, the vile, and the undeserving; but he saves those, sometimes, who are so pleased with their sins, that they do not wish to be any better.

How good was God to answer the prayers of Job,—of Moses, when he prayed for all Israel, of Hannah, of Daniel, of Christ, of the apostles, and of every sincere, broken heart on earth! Oh! there is not a child here who can ever offer a real prayer which God will not hear and answer. You can never raise a note of praise which will not find his ear. You can never heave a sigh in your bosom, or whisper a prayer in your heart, which he will not regard. The seraph who stands in heaven, with his golden wings folded, may be a thousand times as strong, as old, as wise, as great, as good, as any one of these children; but if you will pray to God from the heart, you will as surely be heard as if you were the lofty seraph.

Let me entreat these children *not to despise the goodness of God,*—

By forgetting him. It is said that when a great army came before an ancient city, the inhabitants were saved by *mice,* which gnawed and destroyed the bowstrings of the enemy. And so that city used ever after to worship mice! This was foolish and wicked. But how many receive good things from God every moment who forget him! When you open your eyes, when you move your hand, when you move the tongue to speak, he must aid you. Every time you eat, or sleep, or drink, you enjoy the goodness of the great and blessed God. Will you forget him? Do not abuse his goodness,

By complaining at your lot. But few people in the world are rich, or handsome, or honoured; but all may be happy, if they choose. But you cannot, if you murmur at what God gives you. You will see other little boys and girls better dressed, and some of them riding in coaches, and some of them having better things than you. But should you complain or feel envy? God has been good to you. You have enough to eat and to drink and to wear; friends to love you, a home to shelter you, a Bible to guide you, the Sabbath to instruct you, a soul to rejoice, a God to watch over you, a Saviour to call you his, if you are holy, and the Holy Spirit to aid you to become holy, if you wish.

Oh! children, don't you take the good things which God gives you, and abuse them by being vain or proud of them, as if you were better than those who have less. Don't abuse his goodness by trifling away your precious time, or by living in sin, and disbelieving in God, when he says he will punish the sinner awfully and for ever.

How ought we to rejoice that God, who is so great and so good, governs all things! Men may be selfish, and wrap themselves up in their own little concerns, and neglect to do good. God will never do so. The little flower in the lonely valley opens its blossom, and the little creature, too small to be seen without a glass, creeps into it, and makes it his home; and God is able to attend to his wants and feed him, and myriads more of just such creatures, while at the same moment he is taking care of all the great worlds which he has created, and all the multitudes of creatures in them. And if we live a few years, and do not shut God out of the mind, we shall see more and more marks of his goodness all our life long. And if we are so holy and so happy as at last to reach the presence of God in heaven, and there read his goodness in the gates of pearl, the streets of gold, in the face of every angel, and of every redeemed sinner from on earth, how shall we be amazed at such goodness, and feel like praising and serving the Blessed One for ever!

Once more, my dear children, let me beg of you *to imitate the goodness of God* as long as you live. You will see distress and sorrow often. Have a large heart, and relieve it as far as possible. Don't spare your good things; God did not spare when he sent his Son for our relief. Give even a cup of water, and he will notice it.

You will meet with those who are unkind and unamiable to you— perhaps become your enemies. Imitate the goodness of God, and pass it over. He is kind even to those who blaspheme his holy name. You will find that "it is more blessed to give than to receive." Does not God teach the sun to shine on the evil as well as on the good? He himself waits to be gracious, and spares his enemies, and does them good. Do you do so, and you will find a rich reward. You will find, too, sometimes, that the ways and dealings of God seem very dark, and very mysterious to you; "clouds and darkness are round about his throne;" but never for a moment doubt that his goodness remains with him still, and that he will bring light out of darkness. You must trust him now, while in the morning of life, and all the way through life; and when you leave it, as you all certainly must, still trust in that great and glorious Being, whose name is Love. His hand will then cover you, and his mercy shall never leave nor forsake you.

And now, dear reader, has this little book given you any instruction, or any pleasure? I shall rejoice if it has. Has it in any respect made you a better child? Has it brought the character of God down so that you understand it any better than you did when you began to read? I shall rejoice if it be so. I am now just about to lay down my pen, and you are about to lay down this book. I have prayed to God that he would help me so to write that you might understand; will you also pray to him to give you a heart to know him, to love him, and to serve him while you live? I cannot speak to you in any other way than by my pen; but I feel as if I wanted to take the little child that is reading this line by the hand, and say, "My dear child, God has sent you into this world for a great errand. It is that you may be ready and prepared to go and live with him for ever. But to do this, you must know him, fear him, love him, and serve him. Will you do it?" And now, little friend, farewell. I do not know your name, but I shall pray for you,—and pray that we may meet in heaven, where "the pure in heart shall see God." Amen.

THE END

SGCB Titles for the Young

Feed My Lambs: *Lectures to Children* by John Todd is drawn from actual sermons preached in Philadelphia, PA and Pittsfield, MA to the children of the church, one Sunday each month. A pure gold-mine of instruction.

The College Days of Calvin by William M. Blackburn is the prequel to the little volume you hold in your hand. It will open the eyes of anyone who takes the time to read about the brilliant student who served Christ in College.

Bible Promises: *Sermons for Children on God's Word as our Solid Rock* by Richard Newton. As with all his books light and heat are on every page.

The Child's Book on the Fall by Thomas H. Gallaudet is a simple and practical exposition of the Fall of man into sin, and his only hope of salvation.

Repentance & Faith: *Explained and Illustrated for the Young* by Charles Walker, is a two in one book introducing children to the difference between true and false faith and repentance.

The Child at Home by John S.C. Abbott is the sequel to his popular book *The Mother at Home.* A must read for children and their parents.

My Brother's Keeper: *Letters to a Younger Brother* by J.W. Alexander contains the actual letters Alexander sent to his ten year old brother.

The Scripture Guide by J.W. Alexander is filled with page after page of information on getting the most from our Bibles. Invaluable

Heroes of the Reformation by Richard Newton is a unique volume that introduces children and young people to the leading figures and incidents of the Reformation. Spurgeon called him, *"The Prince of preachers to the young."*

Heroes of the Early Church by Richard Newton is the sequel to the above-named volume. The very last book Newton wrote introduces all the leading figures of the early church with lessons to be learned from each figure.

The King's Highway: *Ten Commandments to the Young* by Richard Newton is a volume of Newton's sermons to children. Highly recommended!

The Life of Jesus Christ for the Young by Richard Newton is a double volume set that traces the Gospel from Genesis 3:15 to the Ascension of our Lord and the outpouring of His Spirit on the Day of Pentecost. Excellent!

The Young Lady's Guide by Harvey Newcomb will speak directly to the heart of the young women who desire to serve Christ with all their being.

The Chief End of Man by John Hall is an exposition and application of the first question of the Westminster Shorter Catechism. Full of rich illustrations.

Call us Toll Free at 1-877-666-9469
Send us an e-mail at sgcb@charter.net
Visit us on line at solid-ground-books.com

Other Solid Ground Titles

In addition to the book *Truth Made Simple* which you hold in your hand, Solid Ground is honored to offer many other uncovered treasure, many for the first time in more than a century:

ADVICE TO A YOUNG CHRISTIAN by Jared B. Waterbury

HEAVEN UPON EARTH: *Jesus, the Best Friend in the Worst Times* by James Janeway

SABBATH SCRIPTURE READINGS *on the New Testament* by Thomas Chalmers

THE STILL HOUR: *Communion with God in Prayer* by Austin Phelps

PSALMS IN HISTORY AND BIOGRAPHY by John Ker

THE DOCTRINE OF JUSTIFICATION by James Buchanan

A MAN OF BUSINESS by J.W. Alexander, John Todd, W.B. Sprague etc.

COLLECTED WORKS of James Henley Thornwell (4 vols.)

CALVINISM IN HISTORY by Nathaniel S. McFetridge

OPENING SCRIPTURE: *Hermeneutical Manual* by Patrick Fairbairn

THE ASSURANCE OF FAITH by Louis Berkhof

THE PASTOR IN THE SICK ROOM by John D. Wells

THE BUNYAN OF BROOKLYN: *Life & Sermons of I.S. Spencer*

THE NATIONAL PREACHER: *Sermons from 2nd Great Awakening*

LET THE CANNON BLAZE AWAY by Joseph P. Thompson

FIRST THINGS: *First Lessons God Taught Mankind* Gardiner Spring

BIBLICAL & THEOLOGICAL STUDIES *by 1912 Faculty of Princeton*

THE POWER OF GOD UNTO SALVATION by B.B. Warfield

THE LORD OF GLORY by B.B. Warfield

A GENTLEMAN & A SCHOLAR: *Memoir of J.P. Boyce* by John Broadus

SERMONS TO THE NATURAL MAN by W.G.T. Shedd

SERMONS TO THE SPIRITUAL MAN by W.G.T. Shedd

HOMILETICS AND PASTORAL THEOLOGY by W.G.T. Shedd

A PASTOR'S SKETCHES 1 & 2 by Ichabod S. Spencer

THE PREACHER AND HIS MODELS by James Stalker

IMAGO CHRISTI: *The Example of Jesus Christ* by James Stalker

LECTURES ON THE HISTORY OF PREACHING by J. A. Broadus

THE SHORTER CATECHISM ILLUSTRATED by John Whitecross

THE CHURCH MEMBER'S GUIDE by John Angell James

THE SUNDAY SCHOOL TEACHER'S GUIDE by John A. James

CHRIST IN SONG: *Hymns of Immanuel from All Ages* by Philip Schaff

COME YE APART: *Daily Words from the Four Gospels* by J.R. Miller

DEVOTIONAL LIFE OF THE S.S. TEACHER by J.R. Miller

Call us Toll Free at 1-877-666-9469
Send us an e-mail at sgcb@charter.net
Visit us on line at solid-ground-books.com
Uncovering Buried Treasure to the Glory of God

CPSIA information can be obtained at www.ICGtesting.com
Printed in the USA
LVOW082138010513

331898LV00001B/6/A